Dr Charles Moseley

Charles Moseley was born and brought up in Lancashire, and first came to the Fens when he went up to Cambridge to read English. After a varied career, he now teaches mediaeval and Renaissance Literature in Cambridge, and attempts to persuade his victims to take this pursuit seriously.

When not in the throes of this activity, he returns to the village and countryside that form the background to this book, and potters about, doing nothing of any particular interest, and talking to people who will listen. He also writes books.

Also by Charles Moseley

The Travels of Sir John Mandeville
Chaucer: The Knight's Tale: a Critical Study
Chaucer: The Pardoner's Tale: A Critical Study
Reach: a Brief History of a Fenland Village
Shakespeare's History Plays, "Richard II" to "Henry V": The Making of a King
Shakespeare: Richard III: A Critical Study
A Century of Emblems: An Introduction to the Renaissance Emblem
'The Poetic Birth': Milton's Poems of 1645
Milton: The English Poems of 1645
A Field Full of Folk: A Village Elegy
Writers and their work: J. R. R. Tolkien
Cambridge Observed: an Anthology
Reading Shakespeare's History Plays

Out of Reach

An elegy for a Cambridgeshire Village

Charles Moseley

G. David:Cambridge
2010

First published 1995 by Aurum Press,

Copyright © Charles Moseley 1995 2010

ISBN 9781906288389

A CIP Reference is available from the British Library

Printed and Bound in the United Kingdom

This edition, revised and expanded, published 2010 by
G. David, 16 St Edward's Passage, Cambridge CB2 3PJ

In association with
Ostara Publishing 13 King Coel Road Colchester CO3 9AG

To the forefathers of the hamlet

Foreword

By tradition, a Foreword allows acknowledgement of debts. Mine are many. Most important, most obvious, are those to the people among whom we lived in the village, and to whom this book is a tribute of gratitude and affection. I hope that what I have written is some memorial for nameless, unremembered acts of kindness and of good. My thanks are also due to my children: for them the first version of the book was written, as a sort of growing-up-and-leaving-home present. Their enthusiasm encouraged expansion and their permission the diffident offering of it for publication. My wife Jenny, whose version of this story is still to be told, has supported me with the same unselfish forbearance that will, I hope, be glimpsed in these pages. Without her, nothing would have been possible.

I owe a lot to Clive Wilmer, Canon John Byrom and Michael Thomas for their sympathetic criticism. Professor and Mrs Derek Bowett and Sir Martin and Lady Holdgate commented enthusiastically on an early draft. They were early, understanding, and always welcome visitors, who knew many of the people in this book at first hand. To Mrs Bess Sargeant, who read part of the manuscript and wrote to me about it with a wholly typical generosity, my family and I owe many debts. Finally, my thanks to Piers Burnett of Aurum Press are profound. His invariably helpful comments saved me from many solecisms, and to his wise guidance many of what virtues this book has are to be ascribed.

Preface to the New Edition

I was quite delighted when my friends, led by Brian Collings, at G. David suggested that they might be interested in printing a new edition of my little book of memories of the village where we have spent so much of a long, full and at times strenuous life. In the first version of this book, *A Field Full of Folk*, I changed a lot of the names, to avoid any chance of giving offence where none was intended, and I (thinly) disguised the village. But of course many people guessed it was Reach, ten miles of so from Cambridge, in the ecclesiastical parish of Swaffham Prior, and it seemed pointless to waste the best of titles any longer.

But it is sobering to read what one wrote some years ago. There is a character in Antonia Byatt's *Possession* who keeps a diary, saying 'I write to know what it was I saw'. All very well: but the fact is that after wrestling with words to try to communicate the multivocal and multisensual nature of actual experience, you are left only with the words: the writing has obliterated the memory into pattern. All that you have is metaphor, the appeal to your reader, your *semblable*, 'Do you see it too? Can you see what I mean?' One hopes... And to write, as one has to, is to know loss, and the fading of the splendour in the grass.

I owe much thanks to those many people who have written to me (sometimes very warmly) about the first version of this book, but especially to G. David, the bookshop known all over where the world is civilised, where all good books go when they retire, when the dust returns to the earth and the books to the shelves that held them. Indeed, one sometimes wonders whether it is to this bookshop that the Psalmist presciently referred when he said. 'Lord, remember David and all his trouble...'

CWRDM, Reach, 2009

Chapter One

We are never satisfied with our memories. We fidget under their weight. We re-pack the load we carry as the way we have travelled lengthens behind us, and shift it on our shoulders so we can bear it comfortably. So I do not know how accurately I remember the dazzle of that sunlit morning a generation ago, in those months between the end of the Chatterley ban and the Beatles' first LP (Larkin had not then written that poem). We had been married a year. I was between jobs, with no certainty a new one would last. We had a child on the way, five pounds in the bank, a new driving licence. Inconsequentially, we had decided that we could no longer stand living in an upstairs flat in Cambridge, the chief feature of our view a crooked clay finial on the gable of the house opposite. Perhaps there was more than what I now remember as an impulse – 'Let's go out and buy a house' - or again, perhaps there was not: youth's folly - and we were very young - takes little thought for the morrow.

Several of our older friends had just bought houses, all at the bottom end of the market. Perhaps that was what gave us

Out of Reach

the idea: This is what married people do.' It was a time when many a hovel was on the market for a song and a load of work. It was a time when estate agents' prose reached new heights of inventiveness, finding sermons in stones and good in everything. (One house a friend had looked at had defeated them, though: all they could find as an attraction beyond the basic measurements was 'door, with latch'.) I cannot remember any of the thoughts I must have had as I walked down to the centre of the town, but odd echoes, the flotsam of the mind, do swim into focus: the bells of the Catholic church chiming the half hour – we were not not usually up this early on a Saturday; the Continental Shop which sold daring and exotic things like olive oil (for cooking, not medicinal use, which is how my Lancashire childhood had met it) and garlic and wines with names like 'Lagrima Christi'; the mix of smells - fertiliser, seeds, layers' meal, hessian sacking - as I passed the open door of Sanders the seedsman. Soon the Taj Mahal, where a hungry undergraduate could, for four shillings, lunch on meat curry and boiled rice, followed by halwa or coffee - not both. (How cosmopolitan that had seemed to a boy from a place where the fast life was represented by a single basement cafe called El Patio, down by the sea-front, selling frothy coffee!) Just near the Taj Mahal, the first estate agent: I see now with absolute clarity the elaborate RAF moustaches of the man who greeted me. (His name, his face, have gone.)Those moustaches have in memory become, for some reason, a significant part of that headlong and only half-willed process that led us to where we are now. He talked with his back turned to me as he riffled through a filing cabinet looking, as he said, for 'just the house that would suit you'. I can see his back now: rather loud Prince of Wales check suit. I can remember the feel of the Roneo'd sheet with its indistinct particulars - I think it is still somewhere in this house (perhaps a future owner will find it). I can remember wondering what I would read ('What am I doing? Is this what one does?'), and nervously hoping he would think my comments showed a knowledge of the world. (Much later, I

Out of Reach

would find myself teaching his son: Time's revenges...)

He could only find one going for anywhere near what we could afford to borrow: and the village in which it stood was, as he said, a bit out of reach. We bought it, of course. We drove the ten miles out to it that morning in a borrowed Morris E, second-gearing round and round a deserted village looking for 'A charming two-bedroomed semi-detached cottage with roses round the door, and large garden with mature apple tree running down to stream fringed by weeping willow trees.' I remember the seductiveness of the idea of that stream and its trees as we were on our way out, anticipating (and knowing even then, I think, that I was fooling myself into seeing what I wanted to see) the cheerful chuckles of the streams of my own north country, while the windscreen seemed full of visions of a garden with great trees under which our child would lie on summer days. And that illusion, and the day-dream, never quite disappeared, even long after we had lived in the house; they grew over the hard edges of our failures and, I am sure, have colourwashed our memories.

It was much smaller than we expected. Moustaches had not lied about anything, though, just adjusted the way things might be seen: there were indeed roses round the front door - so much so that it could not be opened, and the owner had accepted the situation and draught-proofed the door by nailing a collection of old nylon stockings round it. There were two rooms up, two down, a lean-to coalshed converted into a small kitchen and bathroom. At the bottom of the garden an old corrugated-iron privy was shaded by two six-foot willow saplings on the steep bank of what had all the appearance of a drainage ditch. For this was the edge of the fens; the house stood on the last bit of the chalky high land as it sloped down to be swallowed up in the level vastness of the fen.

The early calm brilliance of the morning had given way to an exhilarating westerly wind which chivvied towering argosies of cumulus across the sky. Their great shadows chased across the shining billows of the ripening barley as the

Out of Reach

wind made the grey-green willows stream out their branches nearly horizontal. The stream - the catchwater drain that stopped the water from the high ground running into the fen - was sluggish as only Cambridgeshire streams can be, despite the great wind stirring its surface. The house and its garden were not what we had dreamed that morning. Yet... I can remember no disappointment. I remember us standing at the bottom of the garden, looking out to windward over the fen as if on a shore with a tide of corn swelling towards us, and I think I guessed then that this place was to be part of our lives for a long time.

In the other, mirror-image, half of the cottage lived two old people. Our vendor took us in to meet them, for she owned their house too. 'They're nice' she said, as we slipped through the gap in the hedge that divided the two long gardens, 'and he is an interesting chap: he's been to America.' (As I write that, a sudden memory breaks surface of how big the world used to be.) They lived in the back room, round the Rayburn, rag rugs on the brick floor. Modernisation ran to no more than a single cold tap and a deep pot sink. In the front room, the chocolate-painted fireplace was fringed with a brown pelmet, braiding that had once been gold at its edge, held in place by a line of brass tacks. The occupants were, we were told, to move soon to a bungalow close by, and we were offered their half for £500. We did not strictly need the room, but, again without recognising the consequences, we agreed. And so in that one morning we had set up the train of events whereby we were to soon be not only householders but also landlords, to whom a rent of £5.15.6 was due each Michaelmas and Lady Day.

I can remember nothing of the succeeding weeks except going to see the bank manager and, with a consciousness that I ought to feel it more important than I did - should not my hand be shaking? - signing a cheque larger than any I had ever

Out of Reach

signed before. We had virtually no furniture; we had no money; we had none of the tools or practical skills which, even then, we recognised that we would need. Yet I think we were as unworried as we have ever been. Youth again; or perhaps I see it with the nostalgia of the middle-aged for a time which may not have existed, but ought to have done, when nothing seemed impossible, when optimism was the norm, and the world was in its shadowless morning. We seemed to have one foot in Eden.

We had little to move. The removers sent their smallest van and yet our table and chairs, and box of books, and my parents' second-best bed, hardly furnished it. That diesel engine starting suddenly drove my mind headlong back through forgotten time to the March morning in 1947 when my father lifted me, barely awake, into the cab of the huge removal van and we moved off through the snow banked at the side of the road to the new house by the sea that I had never seen: and to a lunch of dried egg (brown waxed packets) eaten off an upturned tea-chest, the house noisy and echoing as men tramped around it placing furniture, and in the garden - strange, and big - my ears full of the white noise of the sea on that flat Lancashire beach and the salt in the wind pricking the nostrils and tasting the lips. The memory, flooding back as the echo of the brick-floored room was gradually damped by curtains going up and books going onto shelves, suddenly brought home what we had done: our lives had, for good or ill, changed gear, just as that earlier day had marked an irrevocable move from one life to another, opening the road that would bring us to each other. And to the child soon to be born. Looking back along the road, it looks so inevitable: no other way we could have taken.

We were late to bed that first night. I cannot recall why. All I can be sure of is that the momentary solemnness of the realisation of a turning point, which each of us knew the other shared, had passed, for youth does not dwell on consequences. I remember we made a fire - we found some small logs in a wicker basket in the shed - not because it was cold, but because it was our first. We sat on either side of it in our

Out of Reach

two wicker garden chairs, spindly and fashionable, with our little kidney-shaped coffee table, pleased and a little nervous at the role we were half-consciously playing of established married couple with a house. And I think we went to bed rather wondering whether, to play the role properly, we ought not to have a cat to put out. (A Manx kitten soon adopted us.) The prelude really ended with our first waking with the sun streaming into our eyes, an early tractor chugging past, and a nearby cock dogmatically asserting the morning ('Cock a doodle DOOOO!' Time to be doooing). We realised then, I think, that the rest was up to us. The tide was at the flood and we had to ride the ebb.

Chapter Two

We knew nothing at all about the place where we found ourselves. It was not (and is not) a picture-postcard village, though years ago the Post Office used to sell postcards of it. It has no mediaeval church, no picturesque pub, no immemorial elms, no duckpond. Any once-thatched cottages had been re-roofed in tarred corrugated iron. The first approach was over a bare, windswept expanse of ploughland, then over a humpback railway bridge, and past an ugly little council-built farmhouse. Then, passing the concrete-slab council houses set bare and treeless on the top of the hill, you descended a gentle slope past the long Green with a mixed collection of small, mainly brick, houses, several of them tumbledown. The Jubilee Tree, a horse chestnut planted in 1937, was unremarkable except for its being the only really noticeable tree in a village and countryside where, even then, trees had been ruthlessly grubbed up in the interest of just that little bit more profit from the stiff and sticky land. The red sandstone war memorial - the First World War took a dozen men from even this tiny place - and, on the other side of the Green, the ugly little Victorian church caught the eye briefly as you continued down to the Post Office and shop. Next to them was an over-confident Congregational chapel, the heavy pseudo-classical pediment and pilasters shaded by a wych-elm. The roof was going, for it had been disused for years. Continuing, you ended up at the edge of the fen, on a triangle of open ground, looking straight down the lode which the catchwater drain turns into at that point.

The open patch of ground, we learnt later, was a mediaeval hythe built to serve the once extensive water trade: this hamlet existed for centuries as a busy water-head through which its two neighbours sent out and received their goods.

Out of Reach

Up to 1650 sea-going ships could get up, and even into the 1900s barges brought wine, wood, coal, peat and other things to the water-head. But that trade was gone. The hythe was a wilderness of meadowsweet, fringed by bulrushes and reed-mace, with a few crack willows wading knee-deep in the shallow depression which once had been docks. A few years later - how typical of England then! - it became the obvious place to put the village sewage works. You looked in vain for the English village of the chocolate box or the sentimental memoirs, for Auburn or Cranford: the place was down at heel, muddy, somewhat smelly. It was poor. Corrugated iron and planks split out of bog-oak with beetle and wedges made most of the outbuildings; gardens grew no-nonsense vegetables and fruit, and where there were flowers, they grew in rows alongside the Brussels sprouts and beans. Bits of abandoned or broken equipment lay about where they had been left, and each spring embosomed them in nettles. Along the drove near the house, an iron Ransome's plough - the single-furrow type that the happy ploughboy follows behind the white-blazed heavy horses on countless painted plates and biscuit tins - had been left, in the hedge, and a young elm had taken it to its heart. The wood of the trunk had grown round, ingested, the steel of the handles, the parabola of the mould-board.

Villages have squires - or, at least, a richer class of professionals or owner-farmers who try on the role for size. So we thought, and many villages still do. Ours, never more than a hamlet of its larger neighbours, and never an ecclesiastical parish in its own right, did not. It showed. There were no obviously 'gentry' houses, and most of the land-holdings were either rented in a fairly small way or, if owned, rarely extended to more than 40 to 60 acres. You do not get rich on that acreage, even with a boom in agriculture. Expensive equipment like tractors or combines was second-hand, machinery - Ferguson, McCormick, Fordson - retired elsewhere lived on here. Reapers and binders were still used by some, and in those early years I saw sheaves stooked in their rows under the rising moon of August and was not aware of the end of an era. Combines - those there were - were little red things cutting a swathe only some six feet wide, disgorging the grain into two-hundredweight sacks, tractors, some still with metal-lugged wheels, were small: blue Fordsons, with a badge on the radiator of ears of wheat, little grey or orange Fergusons with metal seats. (There is still one running about here.) Several ran on petrol and paraffin: they had to be started on petrol, and then you switched to paraffin. They started up with a cloud of white smoke and a smell like an untrimmed lamp. (Now the survivors are vintage machines, and, gleaming in new paint, are to be seen being taken to rallies. They are still smelly.)

There was still a substantial number of older people who made some sort of a living from a few acres, an allotment, a productive garden: the ground was worked harder than most the modern inhabitants would be able to imagine - or do. Life had been, and was, pretty hard, and there were families we came to know well who had known in harder times how tasty water-rat soup, or stewed moorhen ('Cut the legs off d they don't taste muddy') could be on a hungry stomach. It was a community of intricate family relationships, suspicious and uncharitable concerning its own cousins but united in its distrust of outsiders: a community where, if hatchets were buried, the spot was marked. There was a sort of peasant truculence one associates more with rural France than with a village in the fat south of England, a defensive resentment of the outsider, the improver, the person who hadn't grown up bent with the effort of that stiff land. There was aggressive expectation of being despised: many times people in the village bitterly quoted to me (challenging me?) what they saw as the outsiders' view, 'Country people are stupid.' Outside power structures of any sort, even well-meaning attempts to improve or help, were regarded with Siberian bleakness. The government was always wrong, so was the council. Save for a very few, the Church had ceased to matter except at the rites of passage of their lives.

And the general attitude to the Church was hostility, resentment. This was not uncommon in East Anglia, where in the last century it became too closely identified with power, the moneyed, the landed interest. The bitterness lingered: I remember the old churchwarden of the next village, in which parish this hamlet stood, telling me how in 1910 the vicar's wife had struck him across the face with a riding crop for not pulling off his cap to her. And how, if the squire of that village did not see you in church on Sunday, you found yourself out of a job come Monday. Of course, I do not know the truth of those stories. I only know that old Bert saw them as true, and it is quite possible that they are generations older than him.

Most of the people in the village were simply uninterested in matters of religion. For some, the word 'pagan' would have been exact: it is not many years since I came across a large hawthorn tree in a little spinney outside the village with every branch dressed in strips of red and white cloth at All Saints' Tide. If the village in general professed any religious allegiance, it was to Congregationalism: their grandparents, their fathers and mothers had built the chapel, which during Victoria's reign had had (according to the newspaper evidence) a fair claim to be the centre of the village's life. So many of the older generation had been given names straight from the Old Testament – Adam, Seth, Reuben, Micah, Ezra, Wilfred, Alvah, Asa, Ada, Aaron - that our undergraduate humour expected to find a Starkadder nourished in every bosom. But long gone were the days when evangelical religious enthusiasm ran so high that the local newspaper could report that the first contribution to the building in 1884 of a new Wesleyan Methodist chapel down on the banks of the Cam was 300 farthings, saved up by a little boy. (Six shillings and three pence was more than half a man's weekly wage. . . . The chapel is still standing, just.) But the chapel in the village had long been disused, and nobody really cared. The sons and daughters of those who built it, who turned out for its packed meetings, who dressed in their best for its summer charabanc trips, were letting it fall down. The awestruck pews where connoisseurs had enjoyed variations on the theme of the imminent wrath of God were whitened with the drop-

Out of Reach

pings of the birds that flew in through the holes in the roof. The Psalmist spoke true indeed: 'Yea, the sparrow hath found her an house, and the swallow a nest where she may lay her young: even thy altars, O Lord of Hosts.' For a few years, the heirs of the builders found the pews to be ideal to chit potatoes on, and the memorial slabs in front of the building were flattened to allow tractors to back trailers up to the door over which deep-cut sandstone proclaimed 'Glory to God in the highes'. — 't and Peace on earth' was hidden by a great ivy-tod.

Years later, when it had greatly changed in population and in wealth, I was asked to write a short history of the village. Having done so, I find it impossible now to recapture the passive receptiveness and naïveté of the youth, looking at this strange and mysterious place about which he knew nothing and did not realise that he did not - a youth so overconfident of his powers and so unaware (thank heavens!) of the amused charity (as well as of the scorn) of his elders. My memory of those early days has become inextricably ivied over with things I did not then know. For in time others told me of their memories; I came to read a lot of the old newspapers, recording the doings of this village and others round about. These too are memory of a sort, one version of the complex doings of the ordinary, the unlettered, who have left few other marks on the recorded history of an area. And alien as I was, those memories of the passions and peccadilloes of people I never knew came to be part of my own knowledge, understanding, memory of the place. I came to know, and enjoy knowing, that at such and such a spot on a favourite walk someone I had never met had dipped sheep. Looking at the river now, I enjoy knowing that at the end of the last century a clever horse called Captain used to pull a string of barges and pace himself so as to be able to jump the fences along the towpath without disrupting the tow.

Out of Reach

I came to know, for example, that *Kelly's Directory* for 1883 recorded that the chief crops were 'wheat, barley, turnips and mustard seed' - little change there. 'Letters arrive through Cambridge at 7.00am and leave at 6.45pm' (not now). I did not yet know that the place that everyone said to us was 'a dying village' once had its own branch, the City of Goshen Lodge, of the Loyal Order of Ancient Shepherds, a Friendly Society: King Charles Wells, who then owned our house, was Secretary in 1904. (Now part of the background noise of the mind.) I did not yet know that in May 1904

> 'James Ivatt, labourer... was summoned for stealing a quantity of watercress, value 6d.... Walter Haylock gave evidence as to seeing the defendant and another man take some watercress from a ditch near the prosecutor's house. The prosecutor stated that the cress in the ditch had been sown and cultivated. The defendant, described as a "Very old offender"... was sentenced to a month's imprisonment with hard labour.'

I read of the reopening of the Congregational church on 12 August 1904 - only a short lifetime before - 'with great rejoicing' and 'large congregations' at afternoon and evening services. I learnt that 'there was a public tea in the barn'; and that the choir 'efficiently rendered a capital selection of anthems and Miss Jennings accompanied on the organ.' The restoration drew support - a dollar here, fifty cents there - from those villagers who had emigrated to Rochester and Irondequoit, New York. I had not yet wondered, in this place that for me had not yet a history, why James Ivatt stole, and what drove those villagers into the trauma of emigration to a strange land, beside new waters, where they still sang the songs of Jerusalem, and home.

These memories of events and people, from many sources, reach back into the nineteenth century. Gradually, they came to be our past too, colouring in the world we inhabit. In this book it is partly that subtle osmosis I try to capture.

Out of Reach

Moreover, to be true to that process, I cannot take refuge in the mask of the donnish or sidestep in footnotes. There might have been a book to be written about the village which would properly have begun with a short history, with its geology, its archaeology, its social history and so on. But that escape, attractive as it is, is denied the one who tries to remember: I knew nothing and cared little at the time I am trying to recall. Those other matters will have to emerge, as and when they offer themselves, in the course of this other ramble through the meanders of my memory.

In those first days, but newly planted, we had not begun to feed on the soil in which Chance, or Providence, or whatever, had put us; we saw with the clear myopia of youth, unaware of the complexity of the webs of relationships into which we had wandered, unaware of the tricky subtleties that govern a community. We were so innocent we did not realise we were outsiders, almost the first immigrants into a community with a long memory and a jealous sense of its own identity. For a peasant community is no respecter of degrees, university or otherwise: all it respects is competence on its own terms. And we had no such competence.

Things are different now - perhaps. I remember when we started work altering and rebuilding the house, when we started trying to grow food, people would stop and lean over the gate, or walk in through holes in the wall: 'What y' doing then? I dun't know as I'd be doing it like that, but please y'sel'. Or in our greenness we would be solemnly told, as we tried to clear patches of nettles, 'Eh, tek hold then, nettles dun't sting this month' - and our momentary credulity of such things (it was momentary) gave the old joke new life and, I am sure, was told against us in the one pub left, where the landlord stood behind the bar with his everlasting cup of tea. (Behind him, through the half-opened door to the cellar three steps down, the beer barrels with their wooden taps on

Out of Reach

the cool brick shelf. Long gone.) And now . . . many new folk in the village, many of the old ones from whom we learnt, but who never acknowledged that we had, dead: and I catch myself leaning over a gate as Moira, my new neighbour, wrestles with the garden of her new house built on George's vegetable patch, saying, 'I don't know that I'd do that if I were you', and playing the same tricks on my neighbours' children as old George played on mine. Is this memory, a testament of affection hardly won and hardly given, a half-conscious nod to the shades of the dead? Or is it something subtler, the place imposing its traditions and ways of seeing on one whose roots lie in other fields, where dry-stone walls net down the heaving of the hills? Or have the wide eyes of youth simply acquired the sidelong knowingness of the old codger? I do not know, and I cannot remember how it happened.

Memory haphazardly shuffles moments of time like cards in a deck: a new deal on the turn of a story. To have any sort of honesty to memory - mine, and through mine, the memories of others, as I remember them - I could not write this book without a like shuffling of fragments and anecdotes and time. I am sure the old folk, too, reconstructed their past to tell it to themselves, and to others like me, and came to believe what they told. But we can only carry so much weight on our journey: things are discarded, and we reshape and repack those things we retain. And, discarded, lost in the haze that mists the beginning of the journey, are those youths we were, who could explain so much if we could see them.

The place has changed a lot, at least partly as a result of our lives, and the lives of those among whom we were cast. The way we see it is more subtly, but no less irrevocably changed, unwilled, unconsidered. And our passivity is itself important, for even early on we had that sense of accident, as well as of the need to find a role. When we lit our first fire, I remember us saying that a month earlier we had never heard of the

Out of Reach

place: somehow events had acquired their own momentum. We sat in the garden one evening that first September talking with visiting friends till the stars grew bright, and said firmly - did we believe we had the power? -'Of course, we'll be here for about five years.' We were set - had we but known it - for over a third of a century.

I can remember there was, above all, a sense of being strangers in a strange land. But also of discovery, a new world. Youth, of course, with all its faults, makes its own passport. And there were those who had ruth amid the alien corn, who welcomed us, who gave us the country welcome gifts of a few spuds, mushrooms left outside the back door, or 'that old cock we couldn't catch last Christmas'. (That last was kindly, but not without its sardonic humour at our expense as supposed townies. When we plucked it, with pliers finally, we recognised the bird's venerability - and I think we gained some credit for actually being seen to have eaten it.) At least we never (so far as I know) gave occasion for village merriment as prolonged as that caused by another young couple in the next village. They had been there only a few weeks when a kindly farmer gave them a rabbit -gutted, of course, for one should always clean a rabbit as soon as possible after taking it. It was received with gratitude, for they, like us, were glad of any meat. But it came out later that behind the delight lay a worry: how did you turn this furry corpse with a head and feet into a delicious casserole with cider sauce? They managed: she plucked it.

Memory of those first months is confused. We can recall golden days in autumn, sharp and clear, but the year was drawing in, and we had little time for anything except doing our jobs, decorating the house (badly), and getting ready as best we could for the arrival of Antonia. A few established friends visited - usually not coming again once they had felt the cold of brick floors set in the damp earth striking up

Out of Reach

through shoes ruined by mud. We began to need a fire, and not just at night. (We tried, a few times, to use the little grate in the bedroom as well.) For the first time, we picked our apples. Blades of ice began to appear at the edges of the stream.

Our first January came, and day after day the dry northeast wind raked the fens and turned the soft black soil and the ruts of the droves to iron. It blew straight into the back door, through every gap in the windows, and we could hear it whistling under the slates as we lay in bed. In such weather Antonia chose to arrive. We brought her home to a virtually unheated house; but then every child that had ever grown up in the village had had about the same start. And somehow her arrival broke a lot of ice. The first evidence of this was taking her out in the pram to the single shop, and everybody who met us and saw her for the first time put a piece of silver in the pram: a village custom now gone, I think. Like a dog, a child in a pram is a great instigator of conversation, and as the year warmed, through people stooping and talking, through people looking at her over the hedge, our circle widened out from the house and began to lap up against other people's lives as well. I came in for plenty of sarcastic comment when I was seen planting a birch tree rather than something useful like an apple or a walnut to mark Antonia's birth, but at least people were talking, not troubling to be polite any more. (I would now, I think, plant a walnut. . . .) An advance, we felt: yet, looking back, I am sure there was still laughter behind closed doors or in the pub. Bringing a baby to a village may win some interest, but acceptance depended on other, much more long-term things.

And in those first months as we waited for Antonia and began (I think) to realise what we had done, it was immediate neighbours - Albert and Kate next door, George across the lane, Reg across the road, and Toby and Bess at the shop - who were the circle of our contacts. Kate saved her used tea-leaves to sprinkle on her rag rugs and the brick floors before sweeping, as her mother had done. Old Albert could still be seen between the rows of vegetables on a fine morning

Out of Reach

digging in the contents of the bucket from the pretty little tarred and rose-grown privy. (The smell of Jeyes' Fluid catches the mind.) They were good to us: their life, drawing to its close, passed on something to ours at its beginning, and perhaps in us they saw something of their own youth as I do with young newcomers. I don't know: it's dangerous to interpret from one's own experience. Other people would tell other stories of them, and they of themselves: we saw only a part of their last chapter, we saw the mature trees in yellow leaf and could not imagine the saplings. (Nor does - can? - youth try to.)

Each tried to pretend the other would not approve of generosity to us - after all, we were not only intruders in a house in which they had lived and brought up children, whose double-grafted apple tree Albert had planted in 1926, but also their landlords, and it was not done to be kind to landlords. Yet Kate would lean over the hedge with an enamel bowl of huge Majestics - the standard maincrop potato then - push it at us, and say, 'Don't tell Him.' Or there might be a pot of jam. Albert, more guarded, gradually thawed to the point where he told stories against people I did not know, thus building up in my mind an odd, partial picture of lost episodes in a life with which our own had so accidentally intersected. Then, gruffly, he might thrust a brace of partridge at us: 'She doesn't know.' (And that meant we had to learn how to deal with game - and pride would not let us ask.) Once he saw me making heavy weather of digging with the new spade my father bought me when we moved in, and, having told me it was no good and I didn't know what I was doing (both quite right), he took it brusquely away and came back a few minutes later with a new edge ground on it. Albert's sharpness helped a lot: more than I knew at the time.

Short, still powerful at seventy-plus, with a shock of startlingly white hair that dazzled the daylight when, rarely, he took his cap off, he had a face with all the cautious scepticism of the peasant farmer who has done a little better than the people with whom he went to school. In most small communities you could find men like him who have 'risen' a bit,

Out of Reach

often through sheer dogged singlemindedness; they are rarely without enemies. We saw the mellow fruit of Albert's ripened years; but we soon found out there were those for whom he was still 'Old Scorcher'. He was a careful man: when 'the electric' came to the village in 1953, he still kept the oil lamps, and only had the minimum circuit installed. There was one round-socketed, 15-amp power point, and one bulb did duty for the front bedroom and the cupboard stairs, which it lit only when the door was open.

He owned a bit of land, rented a bit more, had a son to carry on after him, and still liked to think of himself as running the farm. It did not go without saying that his crops were the cleanest, his barley the heaviest, his sows the most prolific and his bullocks the most profitable in the village. We had no means of comparison, but believed him because he said so. (Later, we found that every crop and every beast in the village was of similar, unexampled, excellence.) Once upon a time, in the bad years of the 1920s, he had indeed gone to America to make his fortune. He had worked on farms over there, but found things no better: and, more to the point, he wanted to marry Kate. So he came back, with the reputation of a travelled man. The only tangible memento of that trip was a pendulum clock above the Rayburn stove that ought to have tocked towards High Noon: otherwise, he was apparently unaltered, his trip resolved into a mere episode, simply of farming in a different place.

He married his Kate soon after he came back. When we knew her a hard life had left its scoring upon her. She still dressed her white hair in the bun fashion of the early years of the century; her high brow was like creased vellum above quiet, slightly hooded, grey eyes and a generous mouth. She had the stillness of countenance that comes to many very deaf people, yet her deafness did not stop her on Sunday afternoons playing the hymns she loved on the harmonium in the little front parlour. Through the wall we could hear her singing them, and thoughtlessly found it amusing: our minds were too noisy to recognise that in Kate, and her mis-pitched singing, there was something of the holy. Her deafness

Out of Reach

precluded any real intimacy, any of the conspiratorial warmth of gossip, but that there was an unspoken liking on both sides was clear. Gradually she told us snippets of her early life, shards of a world which she did not realise was so alien to us as to be almost unimaginable: she had no vision of a world outside the things she had known all her life, and no realisation that others did not know the things she took for granted. We can only now begin to imagine what she was describing, as memory fragments our own youth, and as age, reading and hearing others' memories and knowing the land give us a perspective beyond immediate experience.

Born away down the fen, in a little wooden cottage on the side of the Cam, she and her siblings had, day-in, day-out, to tramp the three miles up the lode bank to the school. In the winter months they left home, and returned, in a deep darkness starred only occasionally by lamplight in the window of one of the rare cottages; in bad weather, she told me, they longed for the eye-smarting warmth of the potbellied coke stove to thaw out frozen wet hands and feet, and in winter they always hoped the lode would freeze so that they could skate up to school. (We remember that obese monster of a stove, its iron glowing cherry red: Jenny used to light it for the Youth Club on Monday nights in later years.) And there were no such things as holidays for peasant children: there were always fowls to look after, the sheep to help with - for there were still sheep then - sugar beet to single, potatoes to pick, fields to be gleaned: and autumn saw even the smallest children, even just before we arrived, picking blackberries for jamming and rosehips for sale (to make 'Delrosa' syrup) at threepence a gallon. A hard life. In her old age, she often seemed in her silence to be reliving happiness; she looked back with no resentment or jealousy, and spoke ill of none. She still took pride in her cooking, even when well over eighty, and was famous for her fruit cakes. But it was not only their dark and sticky mystery that drew a constant stream of her children and grandchildren to her fireside.

She was a faithful churchwoman - indeed, it was for her alone that the Vicar continued to hold evensong in the little

Out of Reach

church as well as in the parish church in the next village, for she was usually the only person to go. Her walls were covered with texts, framed and unframed, and one particularly, fly-specked and yellowed, puzzled me: 'Ye are Witnesses!', it shrieked at you over an out-of-date calendar block. Later, I put together what the story behind it must have been. For a few years after we arrived, the Jehovah's Witnesses were targeting the village quite assiduously, and these solemn and argumentative people would be seen going from door to door in their twos and threes at least twice a year. Mostly they got rudeness; but one Sunday when they came I heard, and saw, what happened next door. I was working behind the high hedge between the houses. As Kate opened the door, the talkative one began; the devout one looked solemnly to Heaven, the usual child solemnly held its hands joined in a praying attitude. Kate's smile encouraged the talker, and it remained steady as he reminded her what a sinner he and she both were. 'Yes, yes,' she kept on saying and nodding. 'Yes,' she said as they offered her The Watch Tower, and they went away mightily pleased, convinced that here was a maiden in Israel indeed. The truth was, of course, that kindly Kate had not heard a word they had said. Just such a visit, I feel sure, lay behind that text on her wall.

Albert was much less patient: we could hear him sometimes struggling to communicate with her, and he got irritated. Understandably, I suppose. But their kitchen in the evenings was a place of warmth and welcome, spilling out into the night as you lifted the latch. (And as you closed the door behind you, you pushed the sacking sausage back to stop the draught that came under it.) Albert would be on the side of the Rayburn by the deep pot sink with its white enamel draining board clipped to it, with his collection of Mills and Boon romances that were his sole reading, Kate sat silent on the other side, knitting or with her hands picking quietly at the flowered print apron she always wore. Once sitting there on a winter night, it was difficult to go away again: but you had to when anyone else - usually their son, with his labrador bitch that had a passion for peppermints, and delicately took them from between his lips - came in. The room would not comfortably hold more than three people.

Every fortnight Kate lit the parlour fire, took the galvanised bath from its nail outside the lean-to shed above the double daisies and columbines she cultivated in the border between the clunch wall and the ash path, boiled water on the stove and gave Albert his bath. We could hear him complain if the temperature was too hot or too cold: I cannot imagine her calm face being anything but as gentle and impassive as ever. And a rare gentleness came over Albert's face when he spoke of coming back from America to marry her. I remember being moved as well as embarrassed one day when Albert told me Kate had had a poorly turn, and he had had to put her to bed. 'Do you know', he said, 'I'd never seen her without her clothes before: she is beautiful.' On them be all peace.

Kate and Albert between them controlled a lot of our first impressions of the village - we had no one else to take our bearings by - and it is thanks to them that they were good ones.

Over the months, and years, other figures passing by acquired names, personalities, histories: and became part of our maps of where we were. And we could never, from the first, ignore George. When the magnitude of what lay ahead of us was but only suspected, there, often hanging over the wall, watching, was George. George watched from his gate the day we first came to look at the house; George stood silently looking into the removal van, and getting in the way, as the men brought our few things out; George offered us an apple each by way of introduction on that first morning we woke up in the village.

He was the dirtiest man I have ever known. He and his brother Reg had inherited the tumbledown eighteenth-century cottage opposite and a patch of land across the lane from us. They had no privy, drew their water from the well and later the standpipe in the road in front of their cottage. For a time they got on reasonably well, living in one room and letting the others gradually fall in. But came the time when they had to decide on a headstone for their father, and they couldn't. I never knew why the quarrel went so deep, but it did, and they were never reconciled properly; George thereafter refused any help from his brother, even when he needed it, and moved out into a green-painted 1930s caravan which he parked on the patch next to us. He put his mother's double bed in it, leaving himself just room to have a little 'Tor Gem' coal stove and a table. He planted a false acacia - a 'pod tree' he called it - to shade it, some apple trees, and proceeded for twenty years to live on what he could grow, and what a spot of casual labour in harvest or in sugar-beet singling time would buy him. And to talk to anybody who stopped for more than a minute.

Yet I have few stories from George - not because he did not tell them, but because he was literally incomprehensible to an outsider like me. His Cambridgeshire accent was thick, to start with; it was further congealed by having to escape past a roll-up that was perpetually at the corner of his mouth. But even when you had got used to that, difficulties were not over, for communication depends not just on language but on a set of common assumptions, and George and I did not live in the same world. George had hardly been out of the village in his life; he had never been further than Cambridge save for one trip to Lowestoft in 1923 with a Sunday School outing. He took no paper but the local one, and read that with difficulty. He assumed his world was the only one humanity inhabited. The world outside the village had passed him by without him noticing, so that he hardly believed in its existence; his mental map had contracted - for he once must have known, at least in theory, something bigger - to the immediate surroundings of the village. A large town was inconceivable to him; and he had got to the point where he did not believe the news. He laughed at us all for believing

Out of Reach

that the Americans had landed on the Moon. It was impossible, he said, for if they had tried we should have seen them go right through it, and - pointing to it riding above his pod tree - there wasn't a mark on it. Ever after that, when we had snow, it was George's great joke that it was 'moondust', and he died in the certainty that the world to all intents and purposes ended at Cambridge with a little extension to Lowestoft. The only anomaly in this extraordinary mental atlas was 'The Archers', which he believed in with a seriousness he never gave the news; and every night we heard it from the caravan, loud enough for all the village to hear. Every story George told, every opinion he expressed, was based on a web of relationships and personalities and previous stories, on people that one did not and never could know, on incidents far in the past of the community: without the keys of long knowledge and shared memory, they were locked away from us inside his own vivid recollection. Yet he still told them, and one politely listened, itching to get on with the job he had interrupted - he was a great interrupter, was George - and not knowing how, or not having the authority, to break the conversation off without offence. The happiest days of George's life in the years we knew him were when some of the villagers, concerned at the squalor he was living in and the very serious malnutrition that was beginning to be apparent, got him the job of village roadman. For then he was out and about all day, 'keeping the water running' as he put it, and nobody who moved in the village could escape.

That flat cap, a uniform mud colour, often made our hearts sink when it appeared round the gate or over the wall, for we knew that whatever we were doing would have to stop for at least the next half-hour. 'Oh?' and 'Really?', regularly uttered, were all we could contribute; meanwhile, one took care to stand upwind of George while idly counting the flyspecks on his glasses. He had a dog, a little terrier-like thing, which he adored, which slept in the big double bed with him; and when Jenny came to wash his sheets for him, their greyness was felted with dog hairs. His clothes were never changed: jacket, waistcoat, flannel shirt, open at the neck to

Out of Reach

reveal thick woollen vest, day-in day-out, winter and summer. (The sort of buttoned, scratchy woollen vest I had hated, and been made to wear as a child.) His toilet facilities were negligible - indeed, when he was still living with his brother. 'Mrs Seth' – and more of Seth later - his neighbour saw him peeing outside the back door, and commented afterwards, 'It was the cleanest thing about him.' Once he won a set of towels in a raffle, and the neighbours' amusement was doubled when they were used as blankets. Yet... all this is true, yet as false as it could be. This does nothing to capture how George fits into the kaleidoscope of memory. Let me try again. That dog: vicious to anyone else came near, barking itself to hysteria behind the wire fence round the caravan - it was utterly gentle with him. We never knew what it was called, and I suppose it must have once had a name. But George called it 'Bugger you' so often that it answered to that. 'Come here, bugger you', 'Shut up, bugger you', 'Git down, bugger you'; and it wagged its tail in pure love the crosser George got. Or again, when he was roadman, he suddenly had more money than he had ever known. He bought real cigarettes; he bought meat pies; he began to enjoy life. And he bought, by the pound, 'Quality Street' assorted sweets. He sorted out from them all the toffees, and kept them in the depths of his clothes, and gave them, hot, soft, sticky, dust-covered, to all the children. For George was a kindly soul, who loved children despite a gruff unease with them. All the kids teased him, of course, but even that I think he quite enjoyed. His mixture of annoyance and affection came out in his remark to any who would listen when Jenny, in our third spring, had just brought Justin, a little scrap of life with a yell that made the eardrums flutter, home to a garden full of crocuses and the first daffodils: 'There's that Moseley, like a dog with two tails because they've got a boy, and that's only another little bugger to throw stones at my caravan.'

And George had a place in the village and community that drew kindliness from others more than many cleaner people have, and do. When he was taken to hospital for the first time, we found we missed him, and missed being

Out of Reach

irritated by him; and when he came back, clean, with shining glasses and masses of white hair, we were rather glad when he got back to his comfortable grey colour. And his few jokes became part of the furniture, so to speak: to a child, 'Go tell your mother there's a woman in her house'; to a cyclist, 'Hey mister, your back wheel's going round'; in winter, a mopping of imaginary sweat from the brow and swatting of imaginary flies, in summer, a mock shivering - these became as seasonal, and as anticipated, as conkers in a school playground. And while I can remember as if it were yesterday the irritation I felt at the time George wasted, I also look back on him with fondness, and a feeling that somehow, the world has in his going lost some of its salt. And children still find his jokes funny.

George was not the only one to have less than total admiration for Buzz Aldrin and Neil Armstrong. Just after the moon landings, one soaking morning, I saw Wally Wells waiting for the bus, looking lugubriously out of the wooden shelter. He was very old; he was already too old to go to Flanders when Kitchener's finger threatened. I hardly knew him - he certainly did not know me - but, partly because I knew his father had owned our house, and partly because he looked too weakly to stand until the bus came, I stopped and offered him a lift. Conversation was difficult. So I asked him if he had watched the moon landings. For the first time, something like animation. 'No', he said firmly. They should not have done it. The Bible says the moon was made as' a light to the night, not to go walking on.' And then silence till I dropped him to perform his mysterious and rare errands in the bustle of Cambridge traffic.

Try as I might, I could not identify the passage in the Bible he was thinking about. Perhaps it was a reminiscence, badly garbled, of that wonderful song of thanksgiving beloved of generation upon generation of those who toiled on the land,

Out of Reach

Psalm 104, v. 9. 'He appointeth the moon for seasons, and the sun knoweth his going down', or Psalm 89, v37: 'It shall be established for ever as the moon, and as a faithful witness in heaven' - neither had much to say for, or against, moon landings. But Wally clearly felt there was something blasphemous in what had been done, and the vestiges of his boyhood upbringing of reverence for the Scripture - the newspapers tell me his family were big chapel folk - may have stirred in the depths of his mind. Wally had been neither to church nor chapel for decades, but the old imprint of the Bible as the ultimate authority still stuck.

Like Wally's, George's father had been, according to the old newspapers, a regular speaker at chapel gatherings, noted for his moving and enthusiastic addresses. I can be sure, I think, that his three sons - we knew two - would have received a sound religious upbringing. But I do not know what George, or his brother Reg, thought of God, or of his father's preaching. Neither bothered any church, even in the extremity of their lives.

Reg, George's brother, continued to live opposite in the house they had once shared. He could hardly have been more different. He had a regular job, he ran a car that was lovingly polished every week; his garden was immaculate; his personal cleanliness was obvious. At six every morning, winter or summer, rain or shine, we would hear the initial crash and then the extended rising note of water being drawn from the standpipe into his white enamel bucket, and he had his cold wash outside the back door before throwing the soapy water onto his garden. George, overclothed even in winter; Reg, stripping to his skin the colour of a winter beech leaf as soon as May brought warmer weather. And Reg had been a famous athlete in his youth, cycling twenty miles of an evening to am in a race and then twenty miles back in the dark with acetylene lamps hissing and glaring on his bike. Indeed, Reg was

Out of Reach

of that generation that still remembered the huge effect of the bicycle on English rural life, greatly increasing the distance at which relationships could be formed; and, occasionally, through his speech nearly as opaque as George's, one gathered that those relationships had been fruitful. . . .

I have a photograph of Reg in his vigour, in the village football team, with others I knew only as old men. He is powerful, broad, not a man I'd like to get across. And one looks in the eyes in that photograph of vigorous men, and thinks of what, uncomprehended, lay ahead of them. Suicide in one case.

When, years later, George died, Reg - who was nobody's fool - took advantage of the rise in property prices to sell his tumbledown house for a fat sum on which he could live comfortably for the rest of his life. He got rid of George's caravan, and put a modern mobile home on its site, where he lived for a few tidy and polished years. (He dug up the pink rose that had been George's odorous pride, and threw it on a bonfire: I grabbed a couple of cuttings, and they struck, and now luxuriate in our yard.) And then he too died, and his heirs auctioned on the site all his, and his brother's, effects. On an evening of torrential rain, they were spread out all over the plot of land: their parents gazed up at the darkening sky from foxed and fragile photographs as little pools of water accumulated in the corners of the frames; pictures of long faded Sunday School outings, cricket teams and football teas stirred memories in some of the older folk; teapots and dishes from the turn of the century gradually filled with the rain, as we tramped all over Reg's growing vegetables which Jenny and I had just hoed against his return from hospital. His tools went too - all the accoutrements of peasant life, billhooks, a flail, a surveying chain, scythes, hoes, wheeled hoes, single-furrow seed drills, a bundle of folded hessian wheat sacks. Everything had to go: turn the memories into what they'll fetch, for the dead are dead and love is wasted on them. And some there be who have no memorial. . . .

We bought nothing at that sale.

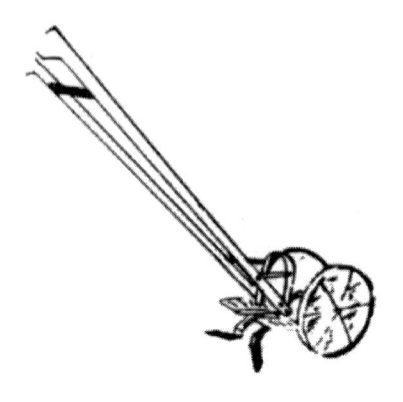

Chapter Three

Let me try to recall the house as we first knew it, as our parents first saw it - to their consternation. With that, let me try to imagine a mindset, now gone, that for Kate and Albert, snug in the house of their memories, was still vital.

The house was utterly run-of-the-mill, typical of the housing that most countryfolk lived in until recently. When built, it had two rooms up, two down, all small, all dark, and cupboard stairs. The upstairs ceilings sloped with the roof, to save the cost of bricks to raise the walls two feet higher. It had a large garden: peasant cottages always did, for the man who built the house was often the employer, and wages could be kept down a bit if the labourer had room to keep a pig, and hens, and grow vegetables. There was a cooking-apple tree (Prince Albert) that despite the hollow darkness inhabited each year by blue tits gave a crop that would 'keep till apples come agin' (nearly). It had a wooden shed, whitewashed inside as a disinfectant measure, where the butter was made: the patent milk separator was still bolted to the concrete floor. Against the house, a windowless lean-to, for tools, and

Out of Reach

storing potatoes, and onions, and apples, and coal (the smell of coal always brings back to my mind the coolth of Kate and Albert's shed). In the corner, built-in, was a copper, a furnace below, a glazed chimney pipe poking through the roof.

That shed epitomised the hard work of running a home, especially with many children, as was common when the house was new. For example, each washday the fire would be lit, and the copper filled with water from the well opposite, or from the river at the bottom of the garden. The backbreaking business started early, for there was the water to draw, the clothes to put in a tub and beat with a posser, either of wood or copper, the rinsing, the mangling, and finally the hanging out (round here a lot used a wire line) in the garden. The line ran along the ash path leading past the rows of sweet Williams and stocks, then the neat rows of vegetables, and the plum and apple trees, to the privy and the river. In the house, one small black range provided heat for cooking: its chimney hook, for a hanging black iron kettle, is still in our flue. (The broken cast iron of the kettle is somewhere in the garden.) And no privacy, no easy chairs, even, and sleeping several to a bed, were the norm. No wonder that courting for the young was an outside pursuit, returning with the warming of the year.

Yet people took a pride in these tiny houses - just as in the back-to-backs of Preston, when I was a youthful conductor on duty on an early bus, practically every woman would be on her knees holystoning her doorstep to a creaminess that stood no footfall. People took a pride in the smartness of their 'good clothes', which appeared only on Sundays and holidays; and people took a pride in their gardens, in their vegetables that made the difference between a good diet and a dull one. They beautified the grimness as best they could, and it was apparent in the way our simple little house and others like it had been treated: a foam of pink and white roses round our door in season, in February the cluster of pink flowers held in the shiny green hollows of 'Soldier, sailor' outside the door, while in summer on the clay tiles of the lean-to shed flowered masses of yellow stonecrop, that

Out of Reach

most welcoming of plants - they call it in some parts 'Welcome-home-husband-though-never-so-drunk'. Along the wall, yellow honeysuckle luxuriated. And in the years of packed ash and cinders round her back door Kate had persuaded giant daisies to grow, close huddled to the ground with their double row of pink and white petals.

The front door had not been used for years, and that was typical too. Everybody automatically went round the back, and the front door was used only for really important occasions, like getting a coffin out. There was a tradition, too, that you never left a house by any other entrance than that through which you had entered. When we had our new front door and offered to let Albert out that way - he had of course come in round the back - the refusal was quite vehement: 'That's bad luck: dew, yew'll never thrive.' Various things I have read since that first faux pas have made me realise that behind the reply lay a whole complex of folk beliefs, but only half-articulated, reaching far back to forgotten times, forgotten people, forgotten houses. But the luck-charm was still, to Albert, potent.

With our first spring, the spring after Antonia arrived, and with many later springs, work had to begin on the house. Though the site had been inhabited for centuries, the present house was thrown up, jerry-built, in 1848, by one Robert Galley, a farmer and warehouser who needed a couple of houses for his men. Bricks from Peterborough, slates from Wales, and pitch pine from Sweden came up the lode; clunch for the bases of the walls was sawn out of the clunch pits on the top of the hill, increasing just that little bit more the enormous hole that five centuries of working that hard chalk had left. (Once upon a time, the clunch for the Lady Chapel at Ely Cathedral had been drawn on sleds by toiling horses up the gentle slopes that led from the cutting faces, and down to the waiting lighter in the dock in my garden: and thence to

Out of Reach

Ely.) Mortar was made with lime burnt on the hill with coal from Newcastle - again, up the lode it came, and I have found lumps of it lying in the mud where it fell off the barges. The house was an epitome of the village's economic life, even to its rebuilding in the agricultural boom years of the nineteenth century.

I knew none of that then, of course, though I was beginning to notice things. All I knew then was that Robert Galley, having fallen on hard times when agricultural prices collapsed, had sold all his properties to King Charles Wells, who had done nothing in the way of maintenance. And, indeed, I do not think he should be blamed for that: no-one would have expected the house to need it or be worth it, for the expectation then was that such houses, cheap to run up, would not last long and that the land would be turned to other uses. Kingie - some still remembered him - made his money from buying cheap houses and renting them; and he made a mint of money, in sovereigns, which his bachelor recluse of a son was supposed to sleep on - or so the story went, as it usually does.

But, look though I did, none of that money, or what it could have bought, went into our house. The Wellses had sold the place a few years previously, and the new owner had put in the small kitchen and bathroom: nothing else. A lot needed doing which it would be tedious to detail, and little of it was easy: there was not a single straight wall or right angle in the place; woodwork had to be treated or replaced, walls had to be removed or built, floors cut out and reboarded. All the wallpaper to be stripped had been put on with flour-and-water paste on top of at least five other layers, the bottom one often newspaper: we found a Daily Mirror of 1920 hiding the subsidence cracks in what became the study. (We stopped to read it, of course: and were struck by the seriousness of its coverage and the elegance of its prose; a gutter press quite free of the implicit contempt for readers shown by the excitable sleazy banalities of modern tabloids.) We tackled that house, and we did not really know what we were doing: but made up for ignorance with enthusiasm and a super-

Out of Reach

abundant energy the joy of which I can just remember. And we got much better at things as we did them, until our later and latest jobs have been taking down and redoing properly those bits we first began on. It is a queer feeling to take apart your own work and remember the first time of doing it as if it was yesterday: to recognise the irritation you felt at the bending of that nail or that bad saw cut, to recognise that at the time you felt that it didn't matter, no-one would ever see it - and now to have to face the failings one had forgotten.

Working on a house is as good as a new baby for making conversation. We were never short of advice - usually implicitly critical of what we had already done. When we were working outside, everybody who passed had to wave or comment: usually with a certain dryness - expected on both sides. For example, I was up a ladder painting the wall, and old Bill Estall went past, not breaking the rhythm of the characteristic lope that years of gumboots and greasy mud develops: 'That's how Hitler started'. And the village knew well the truth of the saying of Confucius - though Confucius himself was unknown - that there is no greater pleasure than to see a tile fall off a roof onto a friend's, or a new neighbour's, head. It had lots of opportunity for that pleasure with the two of us when we began to work on the house and clearly had little idea of what we were doing.

That first winter had a very wet February, when the soil became a quagmire. One night, in the sheeting rain, old Albert came to the door, and complained that the drain outside his back door was overflowing. At first, I could not see why he was telling me; then I realised that if I was his landlord, Albert was jolly sure I was going to sort his drain out. So torches, a lantern, and oilskins, and we tramped off to look at it. Lifting a inspection cover outside our own back door, it was soon clear what the trouble was: the septic tank had filled right up, and sewage had backed right up so that it was level with the top of the pit. At that point, Albert said goodnight and went off to his bed.

It is good occasionally to be thrown on one's own resources, though I could have done without the experience

Out of Reach

on that night of driving rain. I knew where the tank was - weeks before we had asked our neighbour Ben, who lived along the drove over the river, what the funny pipe with a grille on top was, which stuck up out of the ground. (Ben, who had merely leant over the wall to observe these two new people, had stopped to explain about septic tanks.) He had had years labouring in the building trade, and I turned to him - not for the last time - for advice. 'Soakaway's blocked, mate: yew'll have to dig her out.' So I started digging, in the light of a hissing Tilley lamp on top of which the rain spat and jumped. The clay was so wet it had to be scraped off the spade - the one Albert sharpened - and the broken earth at the bottom of the growing hole was islanded in milky water. I went deeper, and deeper, and eventually hit the brick side of the septic tank. By this time, several neighbours had come to have a look. As my spade scraped on the brick, one voice out of the dark said, smugly, 'I told the old lady she should have made 'em put a soakaway in.' The truth dawned: there was no soakaway, and the old lady who put the bathroom and plumbing in had been badly cheated by her builders. And it was up to me to put it right, soon, or we could not use the loo.

I swore, more richly than the people standing round had heard me before - and the village speech used swear words profusely and imaginatively as rhythmic units to give artistic cadence and force to an otherwise unremarkable diction. There was a stirring of satisfaction in the dark. 'Have to dig a trench, mate, and bash a hole in those old bricks,' said a voice - young Albert's, I thought: blast him. So I did, and the trench filled up with half-fermented sewage. But we could now use the loo.

The saga continued for weeks. I was deluged with advice. Finally, when the weather dried up a bit, I was able to excavate a proper soakaway, and a drain pit, and fill the latter with rubble, and start laying the pipes to it. I had told Jenny not to run water, or use the loo, or even move, until those clay pipes were laid and I was out of that trench. And, of course, inevitably, she not only used it but flushed it. I emerged from

Out of Reach

the trench malodorous and discoloured, unable to bath because we could not empty any water till the concrete had gone off, not unreasonably forbidden the house, and not in good spirits. And, of course, Old Albert had heard and seen all from behind the hedge that allowed him to eavesdrop and peep, and within hours the story was all over the village.

Every so often, even after my labours, the septic tank had to be pumped out. The council sent a man with a sludge-gulper lorry to do it, and he ran the pipes out across the garden and down through the crust revealed when we lifted the inspection cover. The motor begins to rev, and the sucking begins. The level drops only slowly, and conversation must be made. He is a nice chap, though inevitably a bit odorous. We talk about gardening, about vegetables, and then we get onto cooking. It is then that he tells us, 'I do all the cooking at home, you know' and as he passes his hand over his face we see his nails black with his work.

Septic tanks were a relatively new thing there, even in the '60s. Buckets were still the norm, and sitting on the bucket on a summer morning, with the birds singing, can be as pleasant as sitting anywhere else. One friend clearly thought so, and often enjoyed a cigarette while contemplating creation. Then came the morning when, incautiously, he put the dog-end behind him, into the bucket filling up with paper. It took a remarkably short time for him to make his exit: there were, of course, several people passing.

Through working on the house, that first spring, we got to know Seth, and it was through Seth we began to send down roots which tapped the rich humus of accumulated memory of the rural world as it had been until the cataclysmic changes

Out of Reach

that the last forty years have seen.

We had of course noticed Seth before, but had got no farther than an exchange of remarks about the weather as he or his friend Stan Webb came up from working down the fen either on their bicycles or on tractors. (One early memory: a hot day, and big red-faced Stan with a rhubarb leaf tucked under the back of his cap to keep the sun off his neck.) Seth's pebble-dashed cottage was opposite: not pretty, just functional: a timber-framed three-room peasant dwelling of the eighteenth century in which, when it was empty and derelict, Seth and his wife had squatted sometime in the Depression years and which he had patiently made weather-tight. A roof, steep for its original thatch, now tiled, dominated the surrounding sheds and a stable made of split bog-oak and tin in which he stored the accumulated junk of many years of many different trades: 'That'll come in one day'.

It usually did, and when he died a man after his own heart took much of it away and kept it for the same purpose. We had seen his stooped figure moving about under the walnut tree that shaded his yard, never idle: splitting logs with slow and regular blows of the axe that is now mine, or methodically, effortlessly, mixing a batch of cement, or cleaning and sharpening tools, or returning, mysterious sack over his handlebars, from the acre of land he had down the fen. Everything Seth touched showed care - the care of a man who made the very best of what little he had got, who had to look after things: his tools were cleaned and sharpened and wrapped up before being put into their invariable places, no weed dared to send up a leaf on his land, and his house was immaculate: the beams gleamed in their new coats of pink or green gloss paint, the stove was freshly blacked, the one copper water pipe was polished to brilliance. I can never now smell the rich, peaty smell of burning bog-oak without being taken back to the small room in Seth's cottage where such a fire burned year-in, year-out under the black kettle.

Out of Reach

I had taken a door out; it was to be replaced by a window. I was making rather a hash of putting the new frame in. An extra hand was needed: suddenly, through the hole in the wall, there was one. Of course, with a practised hand, the whole job now went easier, and Seth had finally begun to impinge on our lives seriously. We realised later that all that wandering about his yard was not because he was busy, but because he wanted to see what we were up to: he hated to see us making false starts and doing things back to front, and was itching to get stuck in. He did; he never from that moment left us alone. I would come back from work, and a quarter of an hour afterwards, on the dot, we would see his door open and he'd make his way across: 'Well, mate, yew cen't sit here all night.'

The point was, I suppose, that if you had been brought up in the hard school he had, you really could not afford to sit down much: a standard of living even approaching the decent meant constant alertness and the readiness to take pains. He helped us a lot - indeed, he trained me, in time, in all the crafts I came in the end to teach my son, and he gave us the confidence to tackle pretty well any building, plumbing or agricultural job. Seth awoke an interest I did not know I had in the techniques of building and crafting. Little by little, as a result of working with him, and listening (I never did much talking), I began to recognise why things were as they were, to take a pride in knowing what tools are and what they do. But we helped him too, and his wife: we sopped up some of his energy, we gave poor Mrs Seth, hardly able to walk through phlebitis, some rest from his fidgetiness. For he was never still, and had been something of a handful when he was younger. Even when he was ill, and knew it, he demolished an old piano, liked the wood, and started making a new bedhead for us and a stool for our daughter out of it. (Neither was finished, and for months we had not the heart to throw them away.)

Seth looked as innocent and harmless as only a elderly rogue can. His hooked nose had the shine and prominence of a cockerel's beak. Narrow-set grey eyes, never more villainous

Out of Reach

than when wide-eyed in innocence, were still keen: he could see, without glasses, a man carrying a hare - and who it was - a mile down the fen. His chin was grey with the smoothness of an old hand's shave. He always wore a checked cap: on its peak, the pattern was invisible under the polished grease of years of his thumb pushing it back. I only saw him without it when he died: he even wore it in the ambulance taking him to hospital after the first of his heart attacks. (The ambulance did a rapid stop fifty yards up the road, and then reversed: we could hear Seth through the doors: 'Bugger it, I can't go to hospital without me teeth!') His face, with its wide mouth, was in repose surprisingly tranquil and kindly, since when he talked, which he did a lot, he was often scornful and sharp. And his talking was worth the listening, for where George talked and one fought one's way through a fog of reminiscence, Seth narrated: he was the hero of his own unheroic stories, but he had a natural gift for structuring a story, and a sense of the irony of his position as narrator. I think he had a gift for fiction too: I hope, in some ways, he did. Seth bulks large in this narrative, as he does in our lives: more of him later.

Those false teeth, like everything about Seth, had a story, which he was happy to tell. He had been to Newmarket one Saturday, and had gone into the dentist with toothache (this was long before the War). The dentist had said to him 'Do you get indigestion?' and Seth had said, 'Well, yus, and I takes bicarb,' and the dentist had said his teeth were getting a bit gappy, and why did he not have them all out - 'Dew. Yew'll feel whoolly better.' So, there and then, out come the teeth. The dentist would have been on piece rates, I suppose.
. . .

Out of Reach

The 1960s was the age of the RSJ and knocking two rooms into one. I got Ben, whom we had only met a few months before but who had volunteered to advise, to help me cut out a couple of lines of bricks at ceiling height in the wall dividing the two front rooms, and we carefully inserted the joist, cementing it in at each end and running a line of mortar along its top to take up the unevenness of the bricks supporting the wall in the bedroom. (All over England, men were doing the same.) Then came demolition of the wall.

This was the first major volume job in the house, and it seemed a pity not to use our friends. We borrowed a tractor and trailer and parked it by the front door: we laid in lots of beer, and we invited them to come and help. It was probably one of the most successful parties we ever gave. Everyone had a hammer, and three of us had shovels, and that wall came down, the kitchen range came out, and their debris into the trailer in double quick time, without the need for trumpets. (A slightly older, more cautious edition of myself would do no such thing: he would clean the bricks of their mortar and their faces of plaster mixed with chopped cow hair, and stack them carefully for future use.) The man who was to be a FRS attacked the fire surround with venom and gusto; the man who would one day run a BBC department picked with an old screwdriver at layers of old wallpaper that had to be removed; the as-yet unpublished authoress threw bricks out of the door, and the stonemason and printer pretended to avoid the death-rays of the child of the QC-to-be, who was convinced she was a Dalek. Yet those cares had not descended on any of us then - need never have done so, perhaps - and knocking down walls was sufficient, and sociable.

For destruction is fun, whatever we ought to think. It is the clearing up afterwards that is the trouble, and we found that out many times as we worked on the house. Sticking a crowbar between the blocks of clunch of the lean-to shed, and heaving, and seeing the wall bulge and crumble was enormous fun, and Jenny and I, to be fair to each other, had to have turn and turn about with the crowbar. But the clearing up was backbreaking, and in the end we got a friend

Out of Reach

with a crawler tractor simply to level the rubble, pack it tight, and we made the garage floor of it: a long business of feeding the gaping mouth of a temperamental old concrete mixer with gravel and cement and water, and carting its vomit precariously along planks to the next bit to be levelled. Jenny's smart businesswoman sister, with the current boyfriend, turned up as we were doing this, covered in dust and with hands rough from cement. The Boy Friend, cavalry twill trousers perfectly creased, insisted on having a go with the mixer - 'giving us a hand'. The two women, one soignée and poised, the other in torn trousers and with hair all over her face, smiled sisterly smiles of envy at each other. Each, I think, thought the other had chosen the better part. As Antonia started crying, they went through the hole in the wall together and left me with the Boy Friend. The Boy Friend stuck the work for about half an hour, and as he drank the last of our beer later said he felt much better for having done some real work, and how lucky we were to have such a quaint cottage to play with. We were glad he did not last long. For we now understood the resentment countryfolk felt when they had been patronised. I think, now, he was trying to be friendly and that we were too ready to write him off because of the vapidity of his linguistic register. But at that time I could gladly have driven the crawler over his brown suede shoes. I noticed they had cement on them. That would be a job to get off. Good.

We knew nothing of how practical things were done. And sometimes were dense to boot. I am glad that nobody ever saw us both that evening when I had Jenny holding up a door frame, more or less vertical, while I laid bricks as fast as I could round it.

And if you build a wall, you have to finish it for decorating. Like all crafts, plastering looks easier than it is. Knock the muck up, twice dry, twice wet, let it go off overnight, knock it up again, Ben had advised, and so I did. That greyish yellow mass in the middle of the floor glared at me, challenging me to get it to turn into a beautifully smooth covering over the new bricks. Must have a float and a hawk,

Out of Reach

Ben said, and I had bought a float and made myself a hawk. I set to work, Jenny watching expectantly, ready to knock up a little more muck as I needed it, for it was not going to take long - she was always better at concrete and cement mixing than I was. It seemed logical to start at the bottom. By the time I had got a layer of the stuff about a foot and a half up the wall, the bottom had begun to bulge, and then gape, and then it peeled off like rolled out pastry and collapsed on the floor. It was a fraught evening, the more so as the plaster was noticeably going off, and we had a large heap of it in the middle of the room, which might be inconvenient by morning. In the end, we appealed to Ben. He was astonished I did not know to wet the wall first, and had the whole lot up in half an hour. I went to bed that night in stiff-lipped silence. But we were, slowly, learning.

A perennial problem with the house, which we never solved in the very early days, was to get it warm. Blissfully cool as it was in a heat wave, in a dank February the cold struck up from the brick floors and congealed all feeling in your feet and ankles. Jenny used to go upstairs to make the beds only after first putting on a coat and gloves. Yet we had both grown up with houses that had unheated bedrooms, where the winter frosts grew foliate patterns on the inside of the windows that lasted all day: one could breath small holes of clarity in them. The in-laws hated the place in winter. They arrived with the car full of suitcases, and huge eiderdowns, and extra blankets, for they were a long way from their efficient central heating. A wide-eyed little Antonia, seeing this arrival, enquired (with some dismay), 'How long are you staying?'

The place regularly froze up. Years later, after one particularly cold spell, followed by a rapid thaw, Jenny summoned me home from work in the middle of the day. She had arrived back from shopping to find water running down the outside

Out of Reach

wall of the house, dripping off the light bulbs, and a disconsolate puppy standing in the middle of the flooded dining room. She was unable to budge the stop-cock. By the time I got home she was baling out: for the level of the floors was below the level of the ground outside. So we took the plunge: we had to have central heating, and this was a job I felt I could not tackle, for I had not yet been taught the ways of pipes and joints. So we called in the professionals.

They arrived in a van that coughed its way to our door. Out got big burly Brian, six feet, sixteen stone and feet like a carthorse. Then comes 'Me Dad': five foot and a hope, flat cap depressed on bald head, thin, an expression that expected that the worst had happened. We came to love those two, for we called them in whenever we had a job that to do that an insurance company would pay for. But at that first meeting we could not see that far into the future. . . .

Central heating? No problem. New boiler? Any day, before breakfast. Price? Unbelievable. When can you start? Next week. So they did.

By the end of the first week we had holes in every interior so that air circulated freely. Copper pipes ran hopefully through them. Plaster and brick dust made trails through each room. A new cylinder had arrived. Things surely were getting on. Then next week Jenny came home to find Barrie with a sheepish expression on his face as he waved a lighted blowlamp apologetically towards her.

'Had a bit of an accident: one or two little scorches.'

In the bedroom half the wallpaper was burnt off one wall, where Barrie had put the blowlamp down as he went to find some solder. The wood in the airing cupboard was partly charcoal where he had enthusiastically soldered a joint in the new pipework. (The solder had dripped onto the floor.)

Me Dad said, 'Don't you worry, Mrs Moseley, that'll be all right. We do decorating too.' So we didn't worry. . . .

Next day I came home to find red 'Hermetite' sealing compound in half-crown size splodges on every floor and every stair tread. Barrie had unknowingly trodden on the tube, and had tramped everywhere. It is good stuff: it does what it says, and sticks, and lasts for many years. We began to be a little tightlipped. But we could not complain about the effort the two of them were putting into the job.

By the next week the holes in the walls were filled, the pipes were jointed, the wallpaper had been repaired, and the boiler had been fitted.

We came home together to find the Turners in some dismay. Me Dad stood in the middle of the room watching, with no optimism, Barrie's large bottom stuck out from the chimney breast while he wrestled with something behind the boiler. There was a tense silence as we came in. Me Dad said, 'Oh, you're back then,' glumly, and did not perform his usual impression of a smile.

'What seems to be the trouble, then?' I asked.

And from the back of the boiler a voice, which echoed up the still-open chimney, said, 'Got the bloody pipes the wrong way round, din't we. I said it wor wrong, but he wun't listen.'

The next day we came home to find the two of them beaming, with a cup of tea ready for us. They had the pipes right now: they had the boiler fitted. They had a fire - such a fire - going in it. The water was scalding. They had won. 'Yew can have y'r bath now, Mrs Moseley', said Me Dad. And there and then she did. With congratulations and much shaking of hands, and a fistful of pound notes, the two went off in the asthmatic van.

Jenny takes a long time over a bath. But quite quickly I heard her getting out and drying herself. She came out looking grim.

'Have they gone?'

'Yes'.

'Better get them back.'

'Why?'

'All the joints are leaking.'

It was true: we checked quickly round the house. The heat

Out of Reach

had opened them, and it was a matter of time before the water, driven round by the new pump, began to run down the walls and drip off the light bulbs again . . .

It was, in fact, the first time they had done any central heating work. But they were good with wallpaper, we could see that, and when we had the next burst, we called them in. And the next. And the time came when little Justin, who had had the advantage of an elder sister to initiate him into the delights of living in an intermittent building site, would follow them round with his little hammer from the toolset that a thoughtful, or mischievous, grandparent had given him, and eat their sandwiches while they were not looking: 'If you grow up to be ten I'll give you a fiver,' said Barrie, looking at a half-eaten egg sandwich. Justin did; and with the single-mindedness of the young, who never forget a promise and never recognise irony, he would have gone to claim it on his new second-hand bicycle had I not stopped him.

Jolly Pat got out of her car across the road. She passed the Cavanaghs' test. 'A good sport, she is,' Me Dad said. I knew a story was coming, and waited.

'We wor laying a bit of new concrete, back of the factory, over the septic tank, and we'd taken the top off of it. 'Course, we'd put sumtin' over it - couple of bits of two by four and sortie ply. Along comes that old gul, and we sez, dun't yew go by that old tank, and she sez "What?" and carries on. Well, she steps right on that ply, and in she goo. Well, we goo and pull her out, and there she is, laughin' fit ter bust. Boy did she niff! So what does we dew? Well, we turns the hose on her. She di'n't half skip!. . .'

Can I ever not think of that story when I see Pat, spruce and neat, on her way to work? I have never dared to mention it to her.

Chapter Four

One of those early summers. My in-laws are staying, a little disconcerted by what their daughter had landed up with but putting up with it with a relatively good grace. (Tea in the garden with cups and saucers, not mugs.) Seth appears, face immobile, broad mouth firm set, stooped back turned to us as he methodically shuts the gate. Pulls off his cap to mother-in-law: 'Afternoon, Ma'am', and begins to make polite and respectful conversation, for my in-laws are, in Seth's eyes, 'gentry'. But we soon get to the point: can I take him down to his land in the Morris Traveller to pick up some spuds? I am only too delighted. . . .

It is a hot day, and I can't guess why Seth is carrying his coat, over a sack, or why he gets into the back of the car. As I back it out of the garage, I hear the clunk of metal on metal. I can't turn round, but try to: 'Do yew keep on, bor.' As soon as we are out of the village, I steal a glance behind me. There he sits, the sliding window open, his gun assembled across his knees, an expression of quiet triumph on his face. 'Do yew stop when I tell yew', he says, as we bump along the drove.

Out of Reach

We get nearer his land. Suddenly he hisses 'Stop!'. A double report, and two partridge stay on the ground as the rest fly away. 'Goo on then, git them - I can't git out.' So my initiation to poaching begins. I jump the ditch, run over the field - I am visible for miles in that flat, hedgeless country -and get the birds. We continue. A hare later, we reach his land, and, sure enough, there are spuds to bring back - about half a stone. For my trouble, Seth digs me a few more, and we set off back, taking aboard by the way some bog-oak he had cut up, a pheasant, some early mushrooms, and a bunch of someone else's carrots.

Mother-in-law, whose father was a notable game shot, is not a little shocked at pheasant and partridge in the second week in August, but is mollified by mushrooms and later eats the partridges without too much repining. Father-in-law suddenly starts talking about his youth in Ayrshire, his time on a sheep farm, and his vestigial accent of the West Coast becomes noticeable. Seth, with a touch of the cap to mother-in-law, melts laconically away, sack over shoulder, dismantled gun under jacket, leaving the day a little warmer than he found it.

That was the first of many such outings with Seth, usually in the old Morris. (When we bought a Renault 4 with a roll-back roof, his eyes gleamed: alas, he did not live to enjoy it.) I was rarely successful at first on my own. Learning to move silently and secretly, to use what cover there was, to know the run of the ditches and the way of wild things took a long time. I was often disconcerted to find when I'd been down the fen (even doing nothing much) very early in the morning that when Seth came across later that morning he'd challenge me: 'And what were yew doing down the land this morning?' It always turned out that someone had seen me, and told Seth; you can't do anything secretly in a small village. It was one of the great milestones of my life when one day I turned

Out of Reach

the tables. I was lying low in a ditch hoping for a chance pigeon, when in the bushes a few hundred yards away on the riverbank my eye caught a movement. I checked that any silhouette I might have was masked by growth on the ditch bank, raised my head cautiously, and watched. Sure enough, out of the leaves came first Seth's gun barrels - they gleamed in the sun wickedly, for the gun was an old damasked hammer gun, innocent of blueing - and then his face appeared. I swear his beak of a nose shone as the sun caught it. I saw the pheasant fall from the tree before I heard the shot.

That afternoon, as we were on each end of a two-handed saw cutting up some bog-oak, I paused to wipe my brow - I had not learnt to keep up his easy pace, and 'let the saw do the work'. Casually, I said, 'That was a nice bird you got this morning, Seth.' The look of plain astonishment was wonderful to behold and savour. 'Bugger me, where wus yew then?' - and then, the smile of genuine pleasure as without a further word we bent back to the saw.

Seth had had more poaching convictions than he could count. Through them, he got to be on terms, if not friendly, at least of nodding acquaintance with the Chairman of the Bench - or, rather, terms where the Chairman, who was one of the largest of the local landowners, nodded and Seth touched his cap. The morality of the game both understood tacitly and clearly. Nobody made too much fuss about wild-bred birds, even though taking them, or hares, without a licence and without the landowner's permission where they were shot or snared was still poaching. Things got stiffer when the actual coverts of the estate were raided, often at night. Poaching on his preserve was a risk the landowner took and no-one questioned that he was entitled to use all means to stop it. If caught, the poacher had his gun confiscated (if he was using one, and heaven knows there are ways of taking

Out of Reach

pheasants without one), and was often fined a substantial amount for those times - many times the weekly wage an agricultural labourer could earn. The risk was high. But, at the same time, it was understood that some poachers poached only to feed themselves and their family, and there was many an instance of the landowner turning many blind eyes to such poaching as long as everyone kept discreet about it. His gamekeeper, who had to enforce the rules, had after all been drawn from the same social group as the poacher, and recognised his own. Problems came when a wet, cold spring, making this soil stick like glue to the feet of weakly young birds so that they could neither run nor fly, had made the new hatch thin on the ground: exactly the circumstances when the gamekeeper was short of birds for the autumn shoots and the poacher's garden was probably producing little and work was slack. Then hunger drove the one and professional pride and a desire to keep his job drove the other - for a good shoot was entirely the work of the gamekeeper. And some poachers, of course, regularly took birds for sale, which was not really playing the game.

So the old folk had many ways of quietly getting hold of a dinner, and sometimes, of several dinners. In the pub in the next village they used to say that every house in this hamlet had a poacher in it. Seth was acknowledged - grudgingly, self-righteously - master of them all. Money had never been plentiful with him, and using the countryside's resources had always been as natural to him as it must have been centuries before to his ancestors. He was up before the Bench a lot, particularly in the hard times of the 30s, but had managed - how I know not - to hang on to his old gun. ('A gentleman's gun, that wus', he used to say: what a lost world that thirty-year-old sentence evokes!) The fine was usually heavy but he always was given 'time to pay'. Did the Chairman of the Bench know how he paid it? I would not be that surprised.

Seth looked at me sidelong. 'Course I paid it. There wor this patch of wheat, and I knew it were whoolly full of these old pheasants. Yew could get 'arf a crown a goo for 'em, then. Used to hop over the wood from Lord F's they did - always

Out of Reach

find a bird in that field. Well, I had a good little old dog then - half terrier, half fox that wor. The little terrier bitch, she went off one day when she wor on heat, and come back looking as pleased as Punch. "Yew've been and done something what yew shouldn't of, my gel," I says, and she jest wags her tail at me and look pleased. Well, dew yew know, when those puppies come they wor all over the place - some red terriers with big brushes, some foxy white things with rough hair. I got rid of 'un all, 'cept this'n. Now that little old dog didn't need no training. It knew exactly what was what. I could take that old dog along of a hedge in Maytime and, dew yew know, that'd pick a pheasant off her eggs as gentle as a mother. Well, then, here I was, twenty quid to pay and fourteen days to find it. So that little old dog and me, we goes off to that patch of wheat, and I sits down by the hedge, and I says "Goo on, then, me ol' beauty" and in he goes, and I keep sitting down and wait. Well, a few minutes and back he come with a good old cock bird, real quiet like. I puts it in me sack, and off he goes again. Well, dew yew know, bor, by dusk I'd got twenty birds in my sack, and that wor heavy. I carried it on the handlebars of me bike next morning to Newmarket, and I sold those old birds all right. Soon paid that fine.'

Pause. 'Trouble is, put all them pheasants together in a sack and they start getting hot, yew know. I reckon those birds must have been half-cooked by the time I sold 'em.' A look down while he rolls a fag, lights it with the huge tin-plate lighter. Then a glance sideways to see how I'd taken the story.

True? I don't know about fact; but true to an image, and a self-image, and handed down as truth. I think Seth believed it. And it was a fact that throughout the year the butcher got little custom from Mrs Seth, and that scavenging cats could always find the elegant bones of birds in his yard.

Out of Reach

Another early memory. A baking September afternoon, the sky so pale blue it is almost white with heat. Absolute stillness. The sweetish smell of really hot ground and vegetation. Not a sound, not a soul about. Seth and I are down on old Harold Sennett's land. (Sennett is an even bigger rogue than Seth. He keeps a punt hidden in the rushes on the lode bank so he can slip over into Wicken Fen Nature Reserve at dusk to knock off a few geese and ducks. As his father did before him.) Right down the fen, Harold's land is black peat, with a peat-digging, half-full of brown water, still in use by Seth and Harold Sennett. We have come down to pick up some ploughed-out bog-oak and some dried peats for Seth's fire. The black ground is hot to the feet; the reaper and binder has cut two swathes round a stand of wheat, and the eye is dazzled by the light reflecting off the exposed straight tall stalks of the standing crop. Not a breath sways those golden colonnades, soaring straight to meet above in the whiter tracery of ears. Yet Seth's sharp eye sees a movement near the centre of the block - no more than a few ears moving when everything else is still, and then stillness again.

'Old hare in there, like as not,' he says.

Out comes the gun from his sack; the damasked barrels clunk into the action, the fore-end snaps on. Two cartridges: as usual, nothing is left to chance, for these are virtually artillery strength, the maximum load. The gun is so old that the barrels are worn bright, the horns of the hammers - it has no safety-catch, of course - rubbed smooth by thumb pressure. Seth cocks it. Then, suddenly, for no reason apparently, he lowers it.

'Here. Dew yew take it. Jest yew walk round the edge of that old wheat and see if he don't put his head out.' He holds the gun out, still cocked.

I am dimly conscious that this is a challenge of some sort, and that it marks something of a watershed. I have never used a shotgun before. I have never killed anything except fish. I am unarguably about to commit several legal offences. And there is not a scrap of cover to hide me from anyone who might glance in this direction. If I hesitate, even, Seth's quick

Out of Reach

eye will notice; if I refuse, I probably lose a certain amount of growing trust, and I certainly get a sneer. I might lose a friend. A refusal would certainly be told against me, and would be all over the village.

I take the gun. The metal already feels hot to the touch, and it bursts into light as the sun catches it. Seth reaches for his tobacco pouch. 'I'll stay here, head off that old hare from coming out.'

So off I go, gun at the high port as I have seen Seth carry it, praying that hare will have the sense to sit tight and not show its head out of the wall of wheat. One side. Now down the long side opposite Seth. Still no sign; but then, two-thirds of the way down, nicely in range, the corn starts moving: the hare is on the move. I freeze. Suddenly, at the base of the wall of gold, there is the hare - just its head, its ears this way and that. But it sees me, and dives back into the wheat. I lower the gun, relieved, yet, somehow, deflated.

We did not get that hare. But in a sense honour had been satisfied, and Seth after that began to teach me more of the things that he had originally been secretive about. He taught me the difference (Oh, blessed difference!) between blackberries and dewberries; he told me the trick for shooting duck in all but the pitchiest of nights - chalk rubbed down the top rib of the gun; as the gun is levelled on the target the white line disappears. He taught me where the mushrooms grew, to walk across a field that was apparently bare of them and go unerringly to where great clusters lurked in their velvet secrecy just under the soil. It is a trick I still have, one that annoys the family so much that a suggestion we go mushrooming nearly always brings refusal. I can walk in their footsteps and fill a bag with what they have missed. And he sold me his spare gun.

I have it still, a heavy old Gallyon side-by-side double hammer gun. Once upon a time I shot a good deal with it, but stopped using it after I was thrown on my back by both barrels going off together. It was a rough old gun, indeed, and after Seth was dead I found out that it became his spare gun when he dropped it in the mud and a tractor ran over it.

(That explained the home-made stock that had been fitted - not without some skill.)

Seth wasn't really doing me a favour, and indeed, some would say he was taking advantage of my greenness. Yet I'm not sure. It was a safe enough gun to him, for this year I've seen one of the best pigeon shots in the area still using something far worse, with pitting in the barrel like a gravel workings. He knew I wanted a gun, and his price was just what I could afford. And the shivers that gun gives me now when I think what I did with it do not hide the keen memory of my bursting pride the first time I went out with it. My gun.

And I did learn to shoot: to take advantage of the momentary glimpse of the quarry as it moved through cover, to be ever alert for a chance, to know the flightlines of pigeons or ducks, and to know the habits of pheasant and partridge - how for example in a frost they will on a morning move from cover onto bits of black earth or tarmac where one can wait for them. (Their feet get cold, poor things', said Seth, 'and it's only kind to put them in the oven to warm them up.') I remember my first hare, shot with a lovely little Belgian folding double-barrelled .410 that fits beautifully in the lining of a coat. A quick, clean kill, an unaccustomed heaviness in the jacket as I walked home., the messy business of butchering soon over, and an extraordinary joy in the meals it provided. No meat ever tasted better than that, sauced with probably the most elementary pride known to man. And, recalling from my Northern childhood a farmer who cured his rabbit skins and used them for rugs and gloves, for years I kept that hare skin, pegged out, scraped and dried, to be the beginning of a bedside fur mat for Antonia. But that was one of those things that never got made, and the moths got to it before she did.

Countryfolk were not - are not - only predators. Sometimes a man would find a couple of orphaned leverets, and bring

Out of Reach

them up. That, I am sure, is the story that lies behind the advertisement in the Cambridge Chronicle for 8 February 1884: 'For Sale: two tame HARES: Any gentleman requiring such to set down in a park will find them real beauties. Enquire of Naaman Thompson, Little Swaffham.'

An old story: 'Dew yew knaow why those old mushrooms grows in circles?' We begin to explain that we do, but we are stopped.

'Nar. . . yew knaow mushrooms only grows where there used tew be 'orses? Well then, those mushrooms, they grow where the stallion used to piss, and when he had finished, he shook his pizzel about, and the drips, they fly in a circle wun't they? and that's where yew'll find mushrooms.'

God bless stallions.

As I finger and weigh these memories, I realise that telling them could too easily suggest a life of mere bucolic roguery. But it was not, and never had been. Seth and Reg and George (when we could understand him) and Albert soon de our naïveté realise that the fen had never been an easy place to live or work. That is why saving and using every liitle thing, why hare skins and poaching, mattered. We soon grew to be irritated if visitors made jokes about Cold Comfort Farm: the country life of the poor was never an idyll.

The fen has an appalling climate - baking and steamy in summer, with an aerial soup of flies and midges that keeps one on the move, and searingly cold or squelchily damp in winter. A wind in spring can cause a dust storm that brings the snow-ploughs out to clear the black drifts off the roads, a storm in which you cannot drive and can hardly walk, where fine, black dust drives through every crevice and puts half-

Out of Reach

inch-thick deposits on every flat surface in the house. Behind the wallpaper, under the floorboards, in the hollows of the clunch walls, as we gradually worked through the house, there was always that deposit of fen dirt; and, with it, the millions of corpses of the little millimetre-long flies that appear every August from the ripe corn and get everywhere, even behind the glass of pictures and in the wax of ears. Yet despite all this, the local folk had an attachment to the land that often seemed even affectionate. They remembered some good times. The old folk especially remembered the hard but not unhappy times of harvest in the golden summers of their childhood before 1914, when the whole village was out getting in the harvest in a race with the dews of dusk. Their memories too were gilded with the setting of their suns. They remembered the trees they or their fathers had planted, the ditches they had dug. To me, they recalled with something of a swagger the hard times when food was short and children were crying with hunger and cold, and jobs precarious or non-existent. They needed to waste nothing: there was never enough food, and butcher's meat was a rare delicacy.

But some wild meats were less favoured than others. We were warned never to heat cooked hare up again more than once: 'Dew, and that'll make feel you whoolly bad.' I do not know why, but they were right. (A hare is 'melancholy and hard of digestion', Robert Burton warns in the Anatomy of Melancholy.) The trouble was that we found a hare too much to cope with for just two of us - they can be hefty beasts - and it was difficult to throw it away. The larger families of an earlier times would have eaten the beast at a sitting.

Walking up from the fen one October morning with a bucket of mushrooms, I met Stan, also going home to breakfast, and we got to talking about food: why not?

'Those old black birds, I loves 'em. Get 'em in a pan with some red beet: they're capital.'

Out of Reach

But this was not wholly leg-pulling, for young rooks - not blackbirds, as I thought - are a dainty dish to set before a king, when taken just fledged. Many a countryman I have met since speaks of rook pie with fondness. Does anyone eat it now?

The river too offered food to those who knew. It was, and is, full of eels, those secret travellers whose odysseys take them to the remotest rivulet from the vastness of the Atlantic. When in winter the river was dredged, as happened infrequently, the mud was often full of them, and the older villagers could remember times when children would be sent out with pails to paddle through the mud for the creatures, feeling for them in the cold grey slime with bare toes; rare good food, and free. The man who drove the drag-line pretty well fed himself on eels and the birds he shot with his old ten-bore that lived in the cab. Some people could remember using an eel-glaive - the fork with four or five serrated prongs which you drove into the mud, trapping the writhing eels between the prongs.

Many people had once upon a time had their eel-grig in the river, a wicker tube trap baited with a bit of rotten meat. Later, the technique of making them of the local osiers ('ozhyers') died out, and they were made of wire netting instead. We found one lying around, and of course we had to try it at the bottom of the garden. I spent half a day mending it. As usual, nobody said a word - just watched. It never caught anything, but somehow it made us feel better, more resourceful, knowing it was there and that it might do. It was a good job we did not have to rely all the time on our intentions and hopes to feed us.

Make do, mend: use what there is to hand. Good land needs

Out of Reach

fences - and last year a field was fenced in the village at a cost of three thousand pounds. But, in the old economy, fencing was never a problem. Old Albert looked at me amazed one morning when he realised that I did not know that a bit of green willow stuck in the ground in winter as a fence post would take root, and very soon be a big tree -and, what is more, a useful tree, that could be pollarded for poles. (Willow is a wood that soon loses its strength, but there is plenty to replace it.) It could even be used for fodder. For animals and birds love willow leaves - they have, indeed, a not unpleasant sweetness when chewed with determination. Our hens - having them was, in time, inevitable - in summer scratched under our growing willows, and would often leap up with a clatter of their inadequate wings and snatch leaves from the hanging branches: I used to cut them armfuls of leafy twigs, for which they would abandon freshly scattered corn. Was it the minute trace of aspirin that soothed their little brains, I wonder? For willow is a natural source of the chemical, and willow-bark tea was still remembered in the village as sovereign for colds and flu.

But that is part of the old country medical lore, which I know little about. Sometimes it was really useful; sometimes merely repulsive, like eating a fried mouse for whooping cough. Sometimes it was optimistic, as when Phil's daughter had a huge stye on her eyelid, and Phil took off her wedding ring and stroked the gold across it - the girl flinching with the pain - three times 'Be gone in the morning.' As it happened it was, but I am pretty sure it had nothing to do with the ring.

And we were a little surprised when my father-in-law, who knew about these things, asked us why we were growing opium poppies in the garden. We had not realised the heliotrope blooms with their dark velvet centres nodding on their pale stalks were just that: they came up each year, and despite their heady smell we quite liked them. With his recognition, another bit of the jigsaw dropped into place. For I recollected one of most learned men I have ever met telling me how, as a young Fellow of King's, he remembered Peck's, the chemist's shop on King's Parade in Cambridge, setting out each market day a box of blue pills, and country folk coming in and asking for 'A pennorth o' comfort', a small brown-paper cone full of these blue pills: opium pills, for the rheumatism and agues that the damp fens bred. And many country gardens grew the poppies, and made their own. Rare stuff for a 'flu, or to quiet a fretful child.

Deep in the peat lay the bog-oaks. They were not just oaks, but pines, and beech, and yew trees knotted and tough, in whose cores, just sawn through with the dulling saw that would now need to be sharpened, I have counted above seven hundred rings - and that after half the girth of the tree has rotted away. Once the basin of the fens was dense forest, the wildwood of England. A rising water-table killed the trees, peat grew over their roots, a great gale felled them, and the deepening blanket of peat silenced even the memory of the rustle of wind in autumn leaves.

Bog-oak - 'that's better than coal, that is' - burns with a clear hot heat, with little showy flame. It burns slowly, it can be smoored at night so that it stays in till morning, and many burned it from a preference we came to share. Splitting - the local word was the old verb 'reeving' - a bog-oak required skill and patience, not just strength to swing an axe, a sledge-hammer, or a beetle. That is not to say it was not hard work. Thomas Tusser, way back in 1557, advised, as part of 'Decembers husbandrie',

When frost will not suffer to dike and to hedge,
Then get thee a heat with thy beetle and wedge.

You certainly got warm with wood - firstly splitting, then sawing, and only then from the heat it gave out on the fire. People were always telling us this with great glee, as we straightened up from the saw, or when they saw me down the fen sweating like a cob with an intractable bit of knotted wood no-one else wanted.

It must be cut and split when wet, for if the wood dries out

Out of Reach

it grows hard enough to blunt any saw. In one big farmhouse a few miles away, indeed, sawing and splitting the trunks was avoided almost altogether in the last century: as much of the tree as would fit into the kitchen was cut off and hitched up to a block and tackle on a beam, and the end swung into the huge fireplace where cooking fires had burned for hundreds of year. And as the wood was consumed, a little more of the tree was swung forward.

But Seth had no such huge fireplace. He split his wood, and taught me to do likewise. Then he sawed it up into pieces exactly eight inches long with the two-handed saw we still have and occasionally still use. Wedges were crucial: iron ones for starting the split, wooden ones for widening it. Wood anyone could work into a serviceable wedge, from anything tight enough grained - unsplittable elm was best; but iron was dear, needed a blacksmith, and was never wasted. One morning Seth asked to be driven over to the blacksmith - a year or two earlier he would have gone the four or five miles on his bike. That forge has been gone for years now, and towards the end of Seth's friend's days his trade was only the shoes of the ponies that new affluence was buying its daughters. But, in the darkness of his smithy there still hung the huge shoes for big draught horses, now never to be fitted to the rasped hoof; the walls held all the tools that the smith (bent and aged now) once used to do all the ironwork - for carts, and hinges, and cooperage and so on - that a community needed. The fire of smithy nuts – anthracite - looked black and dead: but a touch of newspaper, and a few snores from the bellows, and a little patch glowed first red, then too white to look at. Seth gave the smith two great lumps of iron - bits of an old cart axle, I think - and asked him to make them into reeving wedges. The hammer rang on the hot iron as it took its new shape.

The iron wedge is tapped gently into the trunk, along the grain, and as soon as it bites firmly, it can be driven hard with the sledge. Wait between the blows: hear if the wood is talking. For as the wedge forces its way in, on each side of it the grain will open, the water in the wood will be forced up

Out of Reach

from the speckled grain onto the surface, and you will hear a creaking and groaning as if an Ariel is imprisoned. If you give it time, and insert another wedge, and then another, the whole tree will split by its own stress cleanly along its length. And once it has been broken out of the round, which is the difficult part, the same process can begin again on each piece. The temptation for anyone new to the game is to think that the harder you hit the better. But no: 'Little taps', and the wood talking, and a look around, and the job goes much more easily.

The '30s had been a particularly bad time for farmer and labourer alike on the land, and a lot of drained land simply reverted to fen. Between the wars, when farming was in as severe a depression as it has ever known, a lot of the drained fen, the most fertile soil in England, went back to wilderness in a couple of seasons. (It soon would again: and, in 'set aside' parts, is doing.) There was no profit in farming, the ditches were not scoured, the reeds spread over the wetter land, and the birds returned in their thousands. Some folk just gave up: a few seized the chance that hard work and low overheads might just give them. In the next fen, an heroic couple carved a farm that worked - it is there still - out of scrub growth of alder, willow, blackthorn and sallow, and fought a running battle with the water that seeped up every winter through the peat. Old Albert got his start at a time when the depression was so bad that if a farmer was prepared to pay the drainage rate he could have the land rent-free. House prices, too, were low: most rented, for a few shillings a week, and a few just squatted in houses that nobody wanted. And all the while the unwilling flight from the land to the towns continued.

I sometimes wonder whether one of the reasons for the dislike of trees, bushes, water and wilderness - things we regard as precious now - among the older folk in our part of the countryside was the consequence of those times, when

Out of Reach

the land, laboured at for years, went back in a couple of seasons to scrub, water and brushwood, and all the work that had gone into taming it went for nothing. Beautiful they may have been, those great skies reflected in fen pools with water the colour of cold tea, fringed with the delicate shading-in of encroaching willow and sallow: but men and women had few eyes for that beauty when a man would walk ten miles on the off-chance of getting a day's work. Even the drained fen often flooded in winter when the pumps could not cope and the main rivers were already in spate. I have heard of homes that regularly had water at their doors: even, of two bricks set in the fire place to make a fire on, for the water lay inches deep on the floor. The houses sat on their islands of almost imperceptibly higher ground, and as the fen dried out the next spring the soil under them moved and heaved as if trying to shrug off these intruders. Livestock had to be rescued by punt and brought to those slightly higher patches, such as where the silts of meandering prehistoric river beds rose slightly above the peat that shrank and grew lower year by year. There are people alive now who remember sailing a boat over the barbed wire fences.

Few people can resist the chance to talk about their own childhood, their own memories. When, gradually - thanks to Seth, I think - it came to be realised that we cared about the place we lived in and what it had been like, people began to tell us a lot. (I have no way of knowing whether were told was true. . . .) There were men in the village who had known the fen take lives before it yielded - as it had surely done in the very earliest years of the Duke of Bedford's massive projects. The shrinkage of the peat meant that every so often the drains and lodes had to be deepened, or cleaned: and then came the terrible work of 'stubbing out' the watercourse, by gangs of men in tall boots, with shovels, working in the greasy mud behind temporary dams. Sometimes, shrinkage meant that the whole system of drainage had to be replanned, and the pumping reorganised. Where the quiet languor of windmills, creak, swish, creak swish, had once been sufficient, now diesel pumps capable of moving thousands of gallons per hour were considered essential. The present main Engine Drain was put in within recent memory, by hard labour of men with spades. Into it, during the last war, it was decided to drain the waters of the adjacent Burwell fen, and this could only be done by building a conduit under another watercourse. The digging of that conduit cost a man his life when the clay collapsed, and Ben, my neighbour who explained the septic tank to me in those first months, remembered the first horrified realisation that the clay wall was bulging, and then the dull slump of the grey mass onto his mate working below, and the rushing of the water onto the tumbled surface. The sudden silence. It took days to get him out.

Yet those bad hard times were regretted. 'Never so well off as when I had twenty shilling a week and there wor a squire in Swaffham Hall', was said more than once to us. The boy who had been struck on the face by the vicar's wife grew up to be a successful builder, a rich man, a churchwarden. His granddaughter's wedding at the parish church in the next village was a big affair, and all the village turned out to watch. Jenny, talking to one of the middle-aged onlookers, was told: 'It was lovely. It was just like the old days, just like the Squire's daughter getting married.' Her interlocutor was looking back to a world of attitudes now unimaginable, irerecoverable, the impress of which can be just glimpsed between the sheets of the old newspapers:

'On 17 October 1884, Miss Margaret Preston, daughter of the Vicar, was married to Rev. Augustus Manley Winter. The whole village was decorated with 'flags and triumphal arches'; 'The marriage psalm (cxxviii) was chanted by the Choir. . . and the hymns 'The Voice that Breathed o'er Eden' and 'Rest in the Lord' were sung with feeling and expression by the whole congregation. . . .' A 'handsome silver salver. . . bearing the inscription "Presented to Miss M. E. Preston by the parishioners on the occasion of her marriage" ' was one of the wedding presents, and was formally presented at the wedding breakfast by 'the deputation of the poorer members of the parish' - whose weekly wage would have bought but few silver salvers.

'The happy couple drove off to the station amid a shower of rice and good wishes, along a line of villagers on either side, en route for the Isle of Wight. It remains to add that young and old of the parish, both at the vicarage and at the school, were entertained with tea and cake and made to partake liberally of the day's festivities. . . which were concluded by a concert at the Reading Room on the following day filled to overflowing by an appreciative audience. The bridesmaids in their wedding dresses took part in the performance.'

A lost world. We glimpsed something like it, I think, on that happy day in June 1977 when the whole village was en fete for the Jubilee of Queen Elizabeth. People who had not spoken for years found themselves together, talking, on the Green, and there was a pageant, and a fancy dress parade, and a tea for the children, and a beer tent. . . . But that too is history now.

It is difficult to hold on to a sense of how things were, the hardship, as waves of nostalgia break in the mind. But: Charlie opposite, nearly blind with cataracts. Once a sportsman, and still a fine gardener, with a feel for plants. His garden was always a picture - rows of delphiniums, of asters, of gladioli; beds of strawberries, rows of currants, a row of tea roses. But it was a picture he saw only as a blur, and the light dazzled him. Then, suddenly, he had his eyes operated on. He straightened up: he lost years; he walked round to see all the places he had not seen since the keenness of his sight was

Out of Reach

blunted. And he said to us, a shake in his voice, as we stood in the summer dusk looking at the rising of the harvest moon, 'I en't seen the moon for years. En't she beautiful?'.

But for how many, in earlier times, was that rapture denied? We suddenly grasped the importance of some social structures and services we had all grown up to take for granted, as the norm. Not a bit of it: merely an interim.

Chapter Five

Townsfolk construct and brewers promote an ideal - a seductive ideal - of the country pub. According to that ideal, the only pub ought to have been the organ of the corporate memory of the village. But we never found it so: perhaps we remained too much the incomers for it to reveal secrets. It was busy only on Sunday lunchtimes, when the men gathered - no woman ever went on a Sunday (Jenny was very severely warned off the one time she made that mistake by Ezra the landlord, who was always called Wilfred - for reasons I never discovered). Only one woman in the village regularly went there, and years after she died her fame was remembered. Wilfred, standing behind his bar that had only beer, and often only mild beer, was no conversationalist. He stood reflectively, a little lugubriously, with his tea in a florid china cup and saucer, cap on the back of his head, contemplating a world he told none of us about.

One pieced bits together. Wilfred and his brother Punch - we never knew his real name - and their father before them had always lived in the village. He had inherited the business from his aunt. It had always been a poor place; she had been classed as a beer retailer in a *Kelly's Directory* of the last century, which implies that she could not afford a spirit licence. Her clientele would have been the very poor. There had been other more elaborate establishments at that time. There were The Ship, The Bull, and The Swan, there was Uncle Tom's Cabin, and then Black Eyed Susan, supposed to be much frequented by Dutch sailors who came up fro j Lynn, and certainly well placed by the hythe to catch the trade from the river, always busy till the railway came. During the great Cambridgeshire coprolite boom it was busy as never before shipping out the phosphatic nodules, popularly supposed to be dinosaur droppings, from which the ne\y magic fertiliser, superphosphate, could be made. Gangs of itinerant diggers turned the countryside over in that profitable search, and I know that for a short period the diggers actually outnumbered the regular population of the hamlet. But the coprolite boom did not last, the railway came to the two villages whose need for transport had made this hamlet grow in the first place, and the water trade declined very rapidly indeed.

With it, not so gradually, went the population. People moved to the growing towns and the bigger villages to find work, and the village became what it still was when we first knew it - a place where rustling stands of nettles, punctuated in June by the flamboyant creamy palettes of elder blossom, marked where once houses had stood and families had grown up. The service trades all gradually collapsed; the coffin-maker died and was buried by his competitor from the next village; the butcher and baker closed down, and the inns found no trade and reverted to private houses, leaving only Wilfred's watering eyes washed up above a tide of tea.

Neither he nor his brother Punch ever married. Punch was always talking about it even in late middle age, but never actually got round to doing anything. But silent Wilfred, who had evidently never had the slightest intention of marrying, had the reputation of a Don Juan, and sometimes when we came home very late at night the headlights would pick him up shuffling over to the next village, with the same purposeful air that we used to see on the labrador we came to have later, when he had once again defeated our best efforts to preserve his pedigree virtue from a *mésalliance* beneath him. He might just have been going for a walk, of course: but Seth's and others' gossip coloured his greyness in pleasantly in our minds. We thought it funny - youth would - and we never knew what storms and torment, if any, went behind those quiet eyes. Only when he died was there any hint of his stoic power of endurance of pain and fear.

Wilfred said very little about his life, though it was clear what he did say that times had been hard for him and his

Out of Reach

brother when they were younger. One of the few stories ever told me underlined this: making money by catching ducks on the soaking winter fields for sale in Bury or Cambridge market. You set out lots of lines, with baited fishhooks, on the water, and tied all the lines to one place. 'And dew yew know, one time I went to get those old ducks, and as I undo the lines to pull 'em in they all tek off at once and lift me right off the ground.' Well, perhaps; but ducks were taken like that, as well as in more conventional decoys, and wildfowl from the fens formed a major component of the London diet in the seventeenth century, and were still a common sight on Cambridge and Bury Markets until the War. But in their late middle age the brothers were no longer poor. One autumn week they won the pools - I never knew how much, but it was a lot. Their first act was to get on the bus, just as they were, gumboots and all, to Newmarket, and presented the cheque at the bank. They drew out several thousand pounds in cash, and went to the most exclusive car showroom in the place. Punch told me that they had always wanted a Rover 3500, and they had more than enough for it. The salesman, so Punch said, did not believe them when they said they wanted it, and seemed to think it all a joke. But - and here Punch always grinned, pushing his cap back on his curly hair - when they took the notes out of their pockets, he took them seriously.

That car never went far. It sat outside the house year-in, year-out, with both of them a bit too scared to drive it, yet proud of the status they had acquired - in their own eyes at least. The money changed the quality of the rest of their lives not a bit - except that Punch gave much of his share away, and, with characteristic generosity, gave a home to a complete stranger, an unmarried mother with a small child. (The child and Antonia became, for a brief spring, each other's shadow.) There was gossip, of course, and Punch thoroughly enjoyed the ambiguously louche part in which it cast him. For, tied to land-work all his life, he loved to see himself in dashing imaginary roles - the solver of problems the bearer of gifts, the travelled man. He never had the car in a higher gear than

Out of Reach

third, he told me, yet he fantasised about the long trips he said he did in the evenings to Manchester. (Why Manchester, I wonder? What secret charm had that place for him?) They had the car for a few years, and then Wilfred died: of gangrene. He had put a pitchfork through his foot, and it had gone bad. But he had not bothered the doctor - his generation didn't. He had just patiently bound it up, and let it rot until general septicaemia set in. And with his going, the pub died too, and for years the village had none. Punch, left alone, could be seen occasionally, sitting in the car, perhaps with the radio on. He never spoke of Wilfred, or indeed much of himself. The blue eyes above the apple cheeks still twinkled when he saw children, and he often commissioned our two to go 'up the shop' to buy his frequent packets of Rennies. Their reward was one each. His unmarried mother and her child moved away to the town, and he was more alone still. Then one day the children came back to tell us he was not there any more.

With the demise of the pub, the only place where everybody went at some time during the week was the shop and Post Office run by Toby and Bess. Once it had been run as a pork butcher's and general store, and there had been a different Post Office further up the street. There had once been a coal merchant and a forge - the latter a traditional meeting place to chat and exchange news. But the businesses failed or their owners grew old, and by the time we arrived the village was supplied by travelling vans from nearby villages. Where once the bakers from the adjacent villages had delivered, in amicable competition, bread and yeast twice a week door-to-door, now there was only one with a selection of brick-oven-baked bread and sticky cakes.

Twice a week - for not everyone had fridges - this hamlet, like all the communities for miles around, was visited by the spotless van of Jack Hurrell, Butcher and Grazier - not deliv-

Out of Reach

ering orders, but actually jointing and weighing and wrapping for the women who came out to the van. (The van shook and echoed as Jack used the heavy cleaver on the scoured block.) 'Famous Pork Sausages', the van's sliding back door proudly reminded those who could not overtake it when the door was shut: otherwise motorists were puzzled by 'Famous Poges'. He was a figure in many communities and memories, Jack, who always in winter wore a scarf round his neck against the rawness of work in the van; Jack, who liked a whisky for his chest - 'Yes Ma'am, Thank you Ma'am' - and ended his Friday round driving very slowly indeed through the winter dusk; Jack, who in spring brought us gifts of asparagus (still called 'sparrowgrass', as Samuel Pepys called it), and we gave him gifts of mushrooms in autumn and mint for his own lamb in summer - 'Yes Ma'am, Thank you Ma'am'. He was known to be a kindly soul, and many was the dog that welcomed his van and waited patiently, with ears cocked, at the bottom of its steps. Old Remus, aged beyond the lot of labradors, sat and drooled long threads of saliva over his feet. Jack could never resist these appeals, and the scrap of offal, or, for our dog, the big bone my parents would have saved for soup, carried proudly into the garden - a weekly ritual for dog and man.

Jack's great passion was horses. He took neglected horses and made them sleek and smooth, and good mannered, and drove them in immaculate traps and barouches and surreys at weekends and Bank Holidays. A white coat and blue-striped apron during the week, but with those horses Jack wore the grey bowler, the check suit, the plaid rug, and his lady passengers sometimes wore dust veils: the smart driving outfit of the turn of the century. What were his dreams?

Then there was the big Cambridge-blue van of 'Johnnie Call Weekly'. It came each week from Cambridge, and was an event for some of the lonelier and older folk. The little driver, twisted up with rheumatism, asymmetric face under a peaked cap with a white top, remembered their ailments and their families as readily as the small sums they put on tick. He had been coming for years, and though his name was never

Out of Reach

known as any other than that blazoned across the front of his van, he was accepted. The shelves inside his van separated by a narrow passage just wide enough for him to limp down, were stuffed with tinned food, matches, cleaning cloths, candles, wicks for oil lamps, nails, screws, tools, string, needles, thread, rubber sealing rings for preserving jars, coal shovels, galvanised buckets, soap, scrubbing brushes, brooms. At the back of the van was a pump, which dispensed the blue paraffin that many folk still used both for cooking and in round columnar heaters like overgrown top hats. We had two ourselves: wet heat, but heat.

(The smell of that heater triggered a memory as sharp, and uncontextualised, as a glimpse of a distant peak through a momentary breaking of the clouds. Wartime, dark, a room to which my mother and I had (as I now realise) been evacuated, a columnar heater, a brown saucepan with baked beans on it. Mum dashing to the door, and me peering through the lifted curtain to see her embracing this strange man whom I had never seen. My father, still in uniform. I cannot remember what happened to the baked beans.)

Increasing prosperity, in the shape of the car, killed Johnnie Call Weekly, and it killed the other local trades and shops we can now barely remember. The bootmaker from ten miles away no longer came every two months to mend and sell boots. Children stopped wearing the sort of boots covering the ankle with which I had grown up. A shrinking population killed the coal merchant's and rag and bone business that had been run from a yard in the village.

So the shop became the last place in the village where everybody regularly went. Toby and Bess provided a meeting place, where the village retained a sort of community. Here one bumped into Reuben, the last man to wear his hair down to his shoulders in the old fenland fashion; or the door with its raucous little bell would open for old Hawkie who lived in a

Out of Reach

filthy caravan at the bottom of a clunch pit on the hill, and waved a loaded shotgun at anybody who came near; or Don, or Joyce, or Miriam, or Florrie the dwarf. Here news and views could always be had while waiting to be served with a quarter of tea or a few stamps. Toby and Bess played an important role, which they could have gravely misused, but never did. They naturally knew a good deal of everybody's business, both directly through their own job and through what they were told as people gossiped over the little purchases that furnish the excuse for the many daily visits the old and lonely will make to a shop. Both were native to the parish, and knew the families of most of its inhabitants.

The cautious, ironic taciturnity of many of the others was not for Toby and Bess. They talked with warmth and animation, and their major punctuation mark was laughter. Theirs was not a facile, or a cruel, laughter; it was a laughter that welled out of a deep sense, a religious sense (they were both devout) almost, of the certainties of life, that all should be well, all manner of thing should be well, despite, indeed perhaps because of, the passing and temporary horrors. (Years later, I came across Simone Weil's thought that if there were no suffering in the world, we would mistake it for paradise.) They saw life as gloriously and irretrievably comic, even when Toby's diabetes, and later his cancer, was nearly killing him, and his skin problems were so acute that he had to pad himself, wear shin pads, against the bruise that could turn to lesion and sepsis. They told many stories of the village and its happenings, never uncharitably, and always with an eye to the best in people. I found out later that Toby had been almost our only advocate on the Parish Council, when we were just nameless and irritating incomers to some other members, who took our ignorance of their ways, and their importance, as studied and subversive insult.

He had his likes and dislikes of course, and sometimes they peeped out from behind his little glasses. He sold, in season, a few vegetables, and displayed them outside the shop. Our dog, always embarrassing, was seen to lift his leg long and satisfyingly over the sprouts one morning while I

Out of Reach

was inside the shop, and by the time I had got outside the sprouts were well and truly soaked. I went back in, expecting to find an irate Bess and to have to pay for the whole bag. Instead, she had called Toby, and the two of them were helpless with laughter, as much at my concern as at the original deluge. And while the laughter was still gusting, in comes severe old Marge.

'Sprouts all right, Toby?'

'Lovely sprouts they are, dew still on them. How many would you like?'

And before my incredulous gaze, he sold her two pounds with a straight face. And as she went out of the door, he said to Bess, 'Well, no more acid than she is. And she'll cook 'em first.'

(The dog, nevertheless, had acquired a reputation never to be lived down. Years later, when Toby had put in foundations for a new store shed, he found dog footprints the next morning all over the new concrete. Our dog was blamed: 'I knew it was him: it was on three legs.')

They knew most of what went on, and were a calendar of memory. Yearly, the didakois, the travellers who followed scrap and seasonal work round the countryside, came back, and parked their caravans in their usual spot. (John Clare's poem catches them: 'A quiet, pilfering, unprotected race'.) Their vans drew up at the village standpipes, to fill their noisy milk churns with water. Some looked at them sidelong, but Toby and Bess remembered the names of the children, recalled the family's problems, and did something to bridge the primitive gap between the settled and the nomad. And there was a yet poorer class of traveller.

One freezing November night, I saw a fire down the fen, by the old gault digging about half a mile from the village. Curious, I walked down there, along the hedge, to find a middle-aged man, a youngish woman and a baby in arms settling down in the lee of a tarpaulin. They did not see me, or hear me in that wind, and I went back to the village wondering what to do. Jenny suggested Toby; and Toby, to my astonishment, showed no concern. The couple had

Out of Reach

evidently been coming for years - 'tinks' he called them - and knew well how to survive. The big fire I had seen was not meant to last; the rash bavin blaze of twigs and small branches would be put out, and the three would then settle for the night on the warmed ground with the tarpaulin over them. Not to worry, said Toby: they would be all right. And they were. They were in the shop next morning, smelling of woodsmoke and earth, and we saw them year after year. The child survived, the old man still comes, but now he has a van, a knife grinding set, and charges a lot for a job Seth taught me to do myself. His voice is the voice of one with some education. What seas washed him up on our shore I do not now, and a look in his eyes tells me not to ask. Did Toby know? Perhaps.

The old ways, the old trades, the old industries that died just before we came, had left many marks, though it took us time to read them. A rusting but still readable enamel sign on the roadside wall of a little cottage reveals where once you could buy Spratt's Ovals and Puppy Biscuit - the word 'Spratt's' lettered to form the shape of a Scottie. Another little retailer, long gone even when we came. We came in time to see the rails taken up from the railway: end of the line for a dream dreamed by the old Squire and his friends. On 6 June 1884, the *Cambridge Chronicle* wrote of the first trains to run on this branch of the Great Eastern Railway:

> The approach of the train. . . was welcomed with a burst of hearty cheering and much regret was felt at the absence of the Squire. . . in consequence of the illness of his son at Hunstanton. It was this young gentleman who turned the first sod of the line last year and his indisposition has put a stop to the contemplated rejoicings now that the work is brought to a successful termination. The Vicar, the Rev T. Preston, made the

Out of Reach

event the subject of his afternoon discourse on Sunday, taking his text from Isaiah xi, 16, 'There shall be a highway for the remnant of my people' - showing that railways and other like triumphs of engineering skills were blessings enjoyed under the dispensation of the Spirit.

Neither the Spirit nor the railway ever brought the hoped-for profits or prosperity to the villages strung along it - indeed, to all intents and purposes it killed the water-borne prosperity of this ancient water-head and outlet for a landlocked hinterland. While it lasted, it allowed the villages to develop a considerable market-garden industry, and a speciality in cut flowers, for the London market. I have been told it allowed at least one person in the next village to leave his house of a morning, walk through the squire's park, catch the train to Cambridge, and be at his desk in the City of London by ten o'clock. Jobs on it were prized, for they were much classier than the farm work that was all most men could hope for; and it is astonishing to think that, with six trains a day in each direction in the 1930s, a little station could and did employ a couple of porters, a station master, and a booking clerk. The railway provided housing, and working clothes, and status; and the widow of the last station master in the parish told me that it was always resented that her husband had that job, as he was not a local man: he came from ten miles away.

But that jealousy of jobs - and place in the community - is pretty typical of anywhere. So too, I suppose, are the little peculations that arise out of kindness. The railway company had also built, near its station, a pub, the Allix Arms, to accommodate all the customers who never came. (I can just remember it functioning as a pub.) It was sold soon after the line closed, and a friend of ours, back from years in Africa, bought it and converted it. Much later, he found himself in a hospital bed next to an old man who had been a fireman on the line. It turned out that the landlord had been a mate of his, and as he went by the pub, across the level crossing, the

Out of Reach

slow pant of the pistons picking up speed, the steam billowing from the engine under load, he used to kick a large lump of coal - a couple of stone or so - off the footplate into the ditch by his| friend's hedge. Coal was dear. And he got a free drink afterwards. ' . . . and I'd have done the same for you, mate.' Frank, in his hospital bed, had passed the test: a neighbourly sort of chap.

Sometime in the 1920s a man with some vision from the large village to the east bought a motor bus. At a stroke he put the carriers - in 1900 there had been two, going twice a week to Cambridge - out of regular business. (Though Seth, for ample, would still perform errands for people in Cambridge, with his pony, until just before the war.) The business flourished for thirty years. His buses were firmly country buses: their values were country values. They carried adverts, to be sure: but plastered along the side between upper and lower decks was an advert for poultry meal - Ray-o-Vitol - its powers (to produce eggs, supposedly) symbolised by a black and red volcano in eruption. They stopped where and when asked, at the ends of lanes or footpaths. Their weekly schedule was built round the rock that on Wednesdays as many poeple as possible would set off to Bury St Edmund's for market day early in the morning, and return at dinner time. And it was a little firm that ran them: the drivers and conductors were all local people, who knew everybody, and the bus was as much a social meeting place as the pub. (So it had been, I remember, when I was a bus conductor in rural Lancashire.) The buses needed routine maintenance, of course, and so on Fridays there was simply no service.

The firm was a family affair, remembered by the name of the owner long after a more grandiose name had been found for the company. But they went to the wall, and the service was run impersonally by the big regional firm, whose drivers did not know the people they served, and whose schedule was increasingly unsympathetic to the needs of the villages. So people used them less and less, and took to the cars that many could now own.

The fate of the bus service, I suppose, is one more example of how the old self-sufficiency of the English countryside has died. Even this tiny place - a population of five hundred at the turn of the century - had a full range of necessary crafts, and produced goods for sale elsewhere. Seth, for example, was the last of a long line in the village to practise the trade of peat digging. In 1900 three people - Seth's father among them - were described in *Kelly's Directory* as 'turf-merchant': they cut and sold peat out of the fen for firing to the villages round about, and to Cambridge itself. Much of the land right down the fen had been dug over several times for peat - some places had been excavated three spits deep, for there was demand for the high quality peat. The dried turves were moved out of the fen along the lode, and thence into the Cam, on barges stacked high with the light cargo.

Seth continued to dig peat out of the wet, forgotten corners of the fen, and dried it over the summer. Till late in life he had sold it in and around the villages. It burns with a clear glow, and little smoke, and to the end of his days he loved to have a few turves to hand. His own land had long ago lost any deposit of the dense mass that could be cut for firing: it had been dug over long since, and the residues had for too long been loosened by plough and desiccated by the returning seasons. But Harold Sennett, down the fen, had some virgin land, and each summer Seth dug peat for himself and for Harold's fire there.

The tools, like all of Seth's, were clean and sharp, wrapped in sacking, their handles black with the staining of the peat, but worn smooth and shiny by hands as black-stained as they. There was a sharp-angled spade for removing the cot, or top

Out of Reach

layer, to expose the undisturbed bed of peat below. And there was the becket, razor sharp, to cut the neat peats.

Of course, I was roped in. As we drove down the fen that first time, I knew that Seth would grumpily pass me the becket and say, 'Here: dew yew cut some.' And I knew that very soon, he would say, 'Give that here. That's not the way to goo to work': it was part of the ritual of that strange friendship, him proving he was better than the youth: 'Not bad for an old 'un'.

The digging had been opened some weeks earlier, and when we got there I saw that Seth had already set up a good stack of turves to dry, diagonally placed across each other to allow the air to get to them. He began work, standing on the cut surface and cutting down with the eighteen-inch blade. Sometimes the tough white roots of reed white-veined the black mould: those turves might crumble on drying. In the bottom of the working the water had already filled up some nine inches: clear, but brown, and dragonflies paused thoughtfully over it. Seth's neat rhythm cut the turf and swung it up out of the water onto the bank in one neat movement, and even I could see that it was crucial that cut and angle were repeated exactly each time, or the turves would be all shapes and unmanageable - and unstackable – sizes. And then the command came. 'Here: dew yew cut some.' So I took the becket, and tried to stand as he stood, and push and swing as he did, and the turf - a poor rhomboidal thing - fell forward off the becket into the water. It could not stay there, and it could not be picked out with the becket. So I had to stop and step in and fish it out by hand. And the same thing happened with the next. And the next. And I was getting remarkably cross with the thing, and myself, and Seth, who was smiling sardonically and getting his breath back. 'Yer book-learning din't teach yew that', he observed, to no-one in particular. And I knew that my failure would be told to most people by the next day, and that he would not allow me to go on too long, for I was spoiling some perfectly good peat.

That was one of those times when I could have happily turned him into a body in the bog to intrigue posterity.

Out of Reach

The top of the hill was pockmarked with clunch workings, for once - for centuries - these quarries had been a major source of building stone. The deepest of them had for years been used by the Rural District Council for the dumping of household rubbish. It smelt; for years it had been on fire, so that when the wind was from the west the smoke drifted over the village, and if the wind blew up to a gale, the fire grew and the smoke plume could be seen for miles. Periodically there would be the noise of explosions, as the fire reached a sealed bottle or tin, or (later) aerosols. It was home to many generations of feral cats, all spit and claws when approached which lived on the plentiful rats. (Most of the cats, to judge by the total or partial lack of tails, were descendants of one disreputable, boss-eyed ginger Manx tom belonging to the Chairman of the Parish Council.)

It was the sort of place any parent forbids children to play in, and which children equally instinctively love and seek out. And I can see why. Rubbish dumps are interesting long before they become archaeological, and quite apart from the pleasure in all the forbidden hideouts the place offered, there was treasure in what people had thrown away. Justin, aged eight, came back one day stooping under the weight of an old sack full of perfectly usable Kilner jars: we use them still. Another time, when the smell had for a time been particularly ripe, he persuaded me to follow him up there to collect what he had found. Feeling my age, I followed his determined little back, and really rather agreed with him when he proudly showed me the luxuriant crop of tomatoes and marrows growing all along one side of it. For someone had dumped a load of sewage sludge there at exactly the right time. And others soon cottoned on: nobody could sell tomatoes in the village for the next few weeks.

Tomatoes: what countryman did not take pride in his outdoor tomatoes, red Ailsa Craig or Country Girl, or the

Out of Reach

nameless yellow variety that was preferred in the fens? But they are disconcerting and sometimes temperamental things. Toby told the story of how he and Bess had gone away on holiday one warm spring, and came home to find they could not get beyond the door of their outside privy. For the earth closet had been the ideal place for tomatoes to germinate, and they luxuriated up through the seat, rested on the toilet-roll holder, and clambered through the gaps round the door. 'Do? What would you have done? We used a bucket for the next few weeks - had the best crop of tomatoes we ever had'.

I quite believe Toby. There was a practicality about him, and an honesty, that would enjoy both the tomatoes and, in both anticipation and realisation, the story they would make. For him, life often did not need embroidering: the unexpected happened. A shop full of customers one pension day, blisteringly hot, and in comes a naked child - Justin, aged three, who had decided to be helpful to his mother, and had taken it into his head to go up the village to buy some fly spray. Toby told that story till the end of his long life, and his widow reminded us of it on the day of his funeral, when the bells of the church where he had long rung rang the only muffled peal and the only Nine Tailors that it has ever been my fortune to hear.

The prosaic and the holy intertwined in Toby's life, just as, it was said, they intertwined in his parentage: he bore a remarkable resemblance to a previous incumbent of the parish. The village church, no thing of great beauty, was on the site of a fourteenrth-century chapel of which the east wall still stood, gradually crumbling in the weather. The churchyard was a mass of nettles, the only things that liked the soil made by years of emptying the ashes from the potbellied coke-fired stove that warmed the building when it doubled as a day school. (A curate, long dead, remarked in his diary when they built a new school, 'Church now free of day school, thank God!') It needed tidying, so Toby set to work. Down the sides in went roses and cherry trees, and behind the altar, between the east wall and the ruin, in went a crop of Majesties. The Vicar (he too was young like us) tentatively

Out of Reach

suggested that there were more ecclesiastical plants, but was told firmly that they cleaned the land and the crop could be sold in aid of the missionary giving to the Church in Korea.

Toby used to lead the ringing of the bells in the next village. The bells hung in a tower infested by pigeons, which scattered like confetti when ringing began. But they left their droppings behind, on the bells, on the frames, everywhere. It was one of the sights of Tuesday evenings, practice night, or Sunday morning, to see besuited Toby climbing up the hill carrying the broad brimmed straw hat that he always wore on his bald head against the bounty from above.

Many memories of him surface, as churchwarden, as postmaster, as special constable. I can see him dressed in his uniform on Remembrance Day at the red sandstone memorial on the Green; I can remember him twinkling down from his great height from under the peak of his constable's hat at children at the annual fair, his neck and chin rolling over the high collar of his tunic. (A day when the village Green is full of men in unaccustomed, mothball-smelling, chalk-striped double-breasted demob suits, some women unrecognisable with their teeth in.) And I have seen him stern with legal majesty when someone had visited the beer tent with too little circumspection. All this is Toby. Yet it is his voice that haunts the memory most, a fine rich baritone, capable of outsinging the most determined of organists. Lifting up his voice, as the shadows of evening deepened, in the canticles of the Prayer Book service, Toby made a joyful noise unto the Lord. And does so still, I doubt not.

He took his job as warden seriously.

'Forgive me asking, but do you go to church?'

'No', I said, surprised at the question, 'No, don't really feel the need for it.' (Had we really thought out any reasons that we credibly could have given him? No, I think; it was simply the fashion of our generation.)

'Oh, OK, don't mind me asking.'

No more. Yet a few years later we were serving on the Parochial Church Council with Toby, and worshipping regularly. Was Toby's question the pebble that started the landslide? I don't know: but I can remember as clearly as if it was yesterday that I was disconcerted, not so much by the question as by the emptiness of my certainties when asked it.

Our first Christmastide in our own house. It is frosty outside, and our room, with its brick floor, is none too warm. Suddenly, the noise of feet and hushed voices outside; carol-singers, we thought. But no carols ever thrilled us like these, for they were not sung, but played on the Victorian set of handbells Toby looked after. The village children, under Toby, were learning the rudiments of bell ringing. (Those bells were held in trust for over a century from one enthusiast to another as village property: a secret harmony.) 'God rest you merry gentlemen' has never sounded the same since. We invited them in, of course, and gave them cups of coffee and mince pies, and, with a curious feeling that I did not know what was the proper form - was I to play the professional, or the villager? - I gave them a ten-shilling note: far more than we could afford, and far more, I think, than Toby, from his look, expected. We got another carol out of it, which unsurprisingly woke the baby. And then they all trooped off into the frost, Toby's laugh receding up the street, and beams of torches dissecting the dark.

Chapter Six

Most of us are great complainers. The Vicar once said that the nearest to optimism he had ever heard in the villages round about was the repeated remark, 'We're getting through'. And the gloominess of the countryman is rocklike - even, as Charles Benham's poem suggests, self-parodic:

> There's olluz summat. When tha's wet
>   The corn git laid, the hay git sp'iled
> And whan tha's dry the Ian' git set.
>   That fare to make me wholly riled. . .
>
> You want it wet, tha's olluz fine,
>   You want it cowd, tha' olluz mild,
> You want it dry, there's nought but rain,
>   That fare to make me wholly riled. . .

But sometimes it is more serious. The quiet desperation with which many people lead their lives occasionally comes to the surface, raw, shocking. There were a sister and brother, Gwen and Tom. Neither of them had ever married, and after their parents died they continued to live in the same Victorian labourer's cottage in which they had been born. She went out to work as a home help, he worked on the land. She kept the house so clean that the sun wiped its feet before it came in the windows. George took his boots off outside, and was reputed (I do not believe it) to eat his meals in the shed. Year-in, year-out this continued: a house always swept and garnished for company that never came, where potential visitors were dismissed because 'They only want to see what I've got'. George would pass the time of day as he walked by, and in the 1964 election became expansive when he saw a Liberal

Out of Reach

poster in our window - but his liberalism was less that of Grimond than of his fathers who knew Lloyd George, and even Gladstone. Beyond such contact we never knew him; perhaps we should have tried to.

They brought him home on a hurdle, trudging up the rutted drove, breaking the ice in the puddles as they came. He had gone out the evening before, into the east wind and the hard frost, had made his way in the dark down to the flooded old clay digging a mile down the fen, and had broken the ice. Then he had drowned himself. They had to break the new ice round him to get him out.

No-one ever knew why. And what led the barber in the big village to the east, that Saturday in 1904, while in the middle of shaving a customer from our village, to up suddenly with his razor and cut his own throat? (He survived, to stand trial for attempted suicide. He earned some sort of place in the story.)

The ugly red sandstone monument on the Green recorded the names that the Moloch of the First World War had taken. A few of the older men, when we first knew the village, had seen Flanders and survived. Old Mr Sheldrick, for example, at ninety still cycling on his huge sit-up-and-beg Raleigh up and down the village, back straight, Kitchener moustache jutting fiercely into the wind. We never knew him to speak to, though I bought his wife's equally tall Raleigh at a church auction and ride it myself along roads it knows well. What horrors had those blue eyes seen? I don't think he ever told anyone: Remembrance Day brought out his poppy and his medals, but not his thoughts.

How did they cope, those boys from the sad shires of England? More to the point, how did the survivors ever come back again, and settle back into the routine they had left, as they nearly all did? The ones I knew hardly ever talked about the war, though I have known men elsewhere who did. (The

Out of Reach

PT instructor and CCF RSM at my school, ex-regular army, ex-Aldershot training camp, talking to us about the bromide put in Army tea 'to curb your sexual urges, my sons - but it doesn't', or, with glee, about the time he stuck a bayonet in a German's guts and twisted it round.) For the men in the village, mostly, it seems to have been an episode that related in no way to lives lived before or after, and which they had no interest in communicating. Perhaps some realised that there was no way it could be communicated to those who had not shared those years in Flanders.

At the same time, it is worth remembering that not all the soldiers were in a permanent state of trauma, horror and gloom throughout their service. War has huge periods of inactivity and boredom, when nothing very much happens, when men living together find ways of making things bearable. And sometimes even having a sort of fun. Seth was one of the few who did talk - a bit - about the War, always with himself as hero of some more or less disreputable episode. How true these were is anybody's guess. He had been in the Veterinary Corps, charged with looking after remounts and transport mules and horses. A lot of his time was spent doing exactly what he had done at home, without the same sort of crop following the plodding of the horses across the land. A lot of his time, too, had been spent with horses in places like Amiens and Rouen ('Roo-on'). I remember his wicked old eyes gleaming as he told about the good times he had had in Roo-on, and how he had, of course, usually got the better of people. He told me several times - which might indicate his pride in it - of when he had been with a tart in Rouen, and had pinched her takings, while actually sampling her wares, from the top of her stocking where she had stuck them. I think, on second thoughts, he may have told me that more than once because I may have let him see that I found the meanness of it distasteful. Seth was one who enjoyed teasing.

But yarns apart, he never spoke of the horrors of the Flanders mud, which he had seen, or of the carnage of his generation, of the friends of his youth whom he had lost. He never spoke of those names on the memorial he knew and

Out of Reach

was cousin to. The brown trilby came out on Remembrance Day, when he joined most of the village on the Green, and fleetingly, in that communal seriousness, one glimpsed the drawing down of blinds there must have been.

But that generation is now gone, and with them their memories, whatever they were. The last Remembrance Sunday service we went to in the village was thinly attended: two Army people, who had retired here, a few others, and by a very few natives of the village - the Chairman of the Parish Council, some of the older folk, and one or two spinsters, now old, in whose eyes, we thought, we could guess the revived pain of the loss of those names on the monument: the husband who never was, perhaps. And the youths continued playing football, and the couple in the house opposite washed their car through the Last Post, and the builders' transistor continued its mindless Radio One burbling. A world fit for heroes.

The visitors who came to us enthused (in the warmer, drier months) about the delights of rural life. Rapidly we became impatient with this mindless stereotyping of something seen only from the outside. Rural life has never been an idyll: had it been, many countryfolk would have tried much harder to stay countryfolk.

The tensions in a small community sometimes surface to public notice, preserved in the aspic of court reports. In 1894, for example,

> John Brightwell was charged with using abusive and obscene language to the annoyance of Sabina Whitmore on April 8. Sabina Whitmore, Wheelwright, said he saw the defendant....against his house. About 4 o'clock, his wife went to feed the hens and said the defendant called her a ——————— old cow and said killed his cat. He further abused his wife, and used

Out of Reach

most obscene language. Mrs Whitmore, wife of the complainant and Ellen Ball, her daughter, corroborated. Defendant called Esther King . . .who denied that Whitmore's door was open at the time stated. She did not hear the defendant use any bad language. Martin Woollard, Labourer... and Mrs Webb corroborated but their evidence did not agree with the defendant's own statement. Fined 15/- including costs.

In the same year there was a case of 'cruelty to a gelding', bad enough to arouse protest and precipitate a court case in a community where animals were worked hard. There was case of appalling cruelty to children, which even now makes the blood boil. Fights after the annual fair among the traders were common - but that, I suppose, was no more than part of a yearly ritual. But we came to the village with the naïveté of our years and background, and were rapidly, painfully, disillusioned (the only way we could begin to see the real). The seven deadly sins stalked the small village just as they do anywhere else. A small farmer, for example, gets just a little bit more land, ploughs over his boundary just that extra furrow, and gets what others, who are not so fortunate or so daring, call 'land-fever' - here are envy and avarice, and they became epidemic in the farming boom of the '70s. In the middle of the day you could stand in the middle of the Green and not hear the sound of any human activity; yet underneath this sleepy surface the place pullulated. I have seen the white eyes of Anger in many faces, and the sidelong glance that spoke of remembered, shared Lust. I have heard the argued ignorance of Sloth, and the self-consuming heartlessness of Envy. It took years to get any inkling of the crosscurrents of jealousies and hates and lusts and desires, reaching back over generations in an entail of lovelessness, and we never really were allowed to know the whole by anyone; but in time we got an idea - and realised that we had been drawn into the same sort of maelstrom ourselves.

A few trees are planted along the road by someone, to provide a bit of variety, a bit of a windbreak. In the night,

Out of Reach

someone uproots them, and breaks the young trunks viciously in half. I plant a decorative tree on the front of the house. We go away, and come back to find it uprooted and thrown over our wall. Someone puts in central heating, and within a week the local council have been anonymously told for it affects the rateable value of the house. Little things, but suggestive. And then we start to hear hints.

Old Albert takes me on one side, and says, 'Yew dun't want to talk to them Coes too much; a bad lot, them.' The Coes are a major clan in the village, from some of whose members we have had nothing but kindness. Whom do we trust? And then, later, someone has a dog shot, and not killed clean, which drags itself home dripping blood and dying: they blame it on someone we know well, and like. Seth tells appalling stories about the morals and behaviour down the fen of the wife of one of the parish councillors - only told without a twinkle, with some venom (jealousy?): told to hurt. Another old man confides one day, a propos of nothing, that no-one was more surprised than his mother at how like Gabriel Gabriel's son had turned out. A youngish couple make a great fuss of bachelor Reg: they become inseparable - and then Reg reveals that he has made a will, and it is in favour of someone they did not even know existed. They drop him forthwith, and Reg spends days weeping - for he had come to love them. Then Reg points out, maliciously, how unalike the seven brothers and sisters are in one family: and that in all the villages round about there are dwarves, all alike, all about the same age, and that once upon a time there was a dwarf pedlar who used to hawk his wares round the area. Then, behind this tissue of gossip, we begin to notice the bigger divisions in the village: real hatred between two brothers, a territorial division between the clan who live 'up the street' and those down at our (older) end, whom the others hate as 'snooty buggers', families united only in their dislike of those outside their quarrels.

The little meannesses we ourselves encountered were inconsequential - though they hurt at the time. It was the discovery, in our naïveté, that most people, including ourselves, had some pretty nasty streaks that really hurt.

Out of Reach

Some of the stories of the past have acquired a comedy they did not once have. It is easy so to tell the story - as it was told to us - of the well-remembered parson before the War who seems to have been 'in the tradition of the English eccentric'. For him, we were told, services were to be held when the Spirit moved him: and as a consequence 'you never knew when there was a service'. Not surprisingly, congregations withered, and the church began a downward spiral from which it has still not recovered. And his wife filled the gracious Queen Anne rooms of the vicarage with her rabbits, and her hens, and her goats, who multiplied as her husband's flock dwindled. These people did the church no good in the minds of their flock: and behind the humour of the telling was a resentment at ... being let down.

What passions lay behind the odd things, now intriguing or comic, that we stumbled on? Like the time when a fall of soot in the vestry after a storm brought down a sheet of metal, which we thought had been stuffed up the disused flue to stop the draught. But the metal was clearly copper - it rang so on the floor - and when wiped it had paint on it. Washed, it came clean: an early seventeenth-century Dutch painting of the Nativity. We deduced that it must have been given it to the church by a Victorian incumbent who was known to have been wealthy, and a collector of some taste. Someone years before our time had resented, hated, that painting: that passion was now unguessable. Was it the same person who hid away the sword hung up in the church after Waterloo by a former squire, which was only found by chance when the building was painted? In the eyes of those of long memory, who stood round the table with the painting on it, there was trouble: someone they once knew, perhaps now dead, had not been what they had seemed.

After service one Sunday, the Vicar called me and one of the wardens into the vestry. On the table was a green lemonade bottle, of the late nineteenth-century type that used to have a glass marble as a stopper. Its neck had been broken - it happened a lot, so that children could get the marble. There were papers too.

We were busy with re-roofing the church porch at the time. A 'temporary' roof had been fitted over its mediaeval ruins nearly a century earlier, and the bottle had been found built into the wall of the porch, where it had been topped to take the wall plates. We unfolded the creased and stiff paper. The story was all too familiar: the girl seduced by someone powerful, pregnancy, her suicide on the railway line by those idyllic, impassive beech trees. Her family powerless, her father the unvoiced labourer in fear for his job appealing to posterity in his secret anguish in the only way he knew: a time capsule, a bottle cast into the ocean of time with the message: 'Help me curse'. Names were named. The hate, and the pain, spilled out of the broken neck.

We destroyed the evidence. I think we were right.

Old Albert and I stood talking over his gate. We could see young Ted doing something to his second-hand combine, which had again broken down, on the far side of his half-cut wheat field which marched with Albert's line of grown-out willows, once a cheap fence. His pretty wife was sitting with her new son in the sunny margin of the field, where she had laid a cloth, and on it the food and drink her grandmother would have called her man's dockey. Albert's blue eyes looked at Ted in silence for a bit. Then he cleared his throat. 'He's just a messer, that one: he'll never make it' - said with venom. Why? Was it jealousy of his youth, and vigour, and family? Or what?

Even those we trusted surprised occasionally. We had not n in the house long - in fact, it was our first summer. Over the

Out of Reach

hedge, we could see the waxen gleam of Albert's strawberries slowly blushing to ripeness under the net he had carefully spread over them. Royal Sovereign: he gave runners to Charlie, who grew a fine bed from them, and Charlie eventually gave some to me, and I have them still. A sweet and delicious strawberry, which blackbirds adore.

Jenny told me the story when I got home that evening. She had been out to peg out the nappies, and had looked over the hedge to see how the strawberries were that morning. A cock blackbird had got himself caught in the net and was fluttering in obvious distress, so she slipped through the gap in the hedge to tell Albert. Out he came, even for so small an errand putting his cap on his white head in the automatic gesture we both already knew so well. With infinite patience, as Jenny watched, he disentangled the terrified bird. And wrung its neck.

Kate and Albert moved out of the other half of the cottage just before our second Michaelmas, and solemnly paid us the half-year's rent before they went. Their children came to help them, and in the course of the morning their possessions were carried across the river to the bungalow they had built

In the afternoon, the children came over again, with bucket and spades, and dug over the entire garden, removing every bulb, every plant they could find. When we went into the empty half that evening, to size up the conversion job that we were to tackle, we found that every light bulb, every coat hook even, had been removed. None of this mattered materially; indeed, we found it in a way funny. But it was the sudden ungenerosity in those who had been so generous that bit deep. (Yet, even as I write this, I think I have understood, after all these years, for the first time: could it have been simply that you always took everything you owned from a rented property? Could it have been that the children knew their parents loved their plants, and wanted to make their

Out of Reach

new home as like the old as they could?) Even so, later, another neighbour told us, with some relish, that old Albert had said how he hated me. Did he? And did he say it? I shall never know. But though we often met, and he was his usual there was a cloud over the way I saw him from then on.

Yet I would not commit the sin of Ham. The faults are those of any community, any individual: it was the expectation that things would be different because of a place that was, and is, wrong, and prevents the real understanding of the human. Even in all this spoiled Eden, we learnt of the transfiguring kindness that can surface in the most unlikely places. During the war many families had had children from he East End billeted on them as evacuees, and many had by all accounts arrived as almost wild animals - dirty, lousy, half-starved, uncontrollable. Some refused milk because it did not come out of a bottle but out of a cow; some did not know what eggs were; some retired into a vicious isolation and resisted any attempt at contact. Yet the old matriarch of the assortment of unlike children, loathed by Albert, feared even by Seth, proved capable of winning these children round, of cleaning them up, of getting them to work, and eat, and behave like children. Toby and Bess took in two little girls, whose father was in the Army and whose mother had been bombed out, and a lifelong affection between the two families developed which warmed all who came near. And we benefited, too, from kind deeds in unexpected places. The person whom most people warned me about was, after all, Seth. Yet many of the women had loved him at one time or another.

We all look different at different places in this masked dance to Time's tune. What stories are told of us, stories we never intended?

If this memoir ran true to convention, I suppose, it would have a fair admixture of steamy sex amid the straw, of rogering among the ricks. It cannot do so and still remain, in whatever sense, true. Doubtless, in the secret and not-so-secret lives with which ours intersected, copulation thrived – when did it not? - but we were too much of the outside to be let into this part of the gossip of the village. We heard hints, it is true, about one of the houses up the street. Some of the men who, now middle-aged, wore their ex-army overcoats to keep off the weather on their open tractors might talk with a distant look in their eyes of the days during the war, when a flood of rapidly emancipated young women came to work the land in the absence in the forces of all but the essential men. (And there were more hedges and barns down the fen then.) We came to know that some now elderly couples had never had benefit of clergy - but then in the remoter parts of the fens years ago, how could they before settling down to raise a family? We heard, from Seth, and Albert of the peripatetic dwarf being caught *in flagrante delicto* - 'fragrant delight' was how Seth remembered the phrase from case reports in *The News of the World* — with one of the matriarchs of the village, and we heard of impossible goings on down the most unromantic fen. All these tales were, I am sure, embroidered.

More trustworthy, more moving, were the glimpses of the youth of those we young had never considered to have felt the like passions with ourselves. Gwen Warren, with her grown-up sons and daughter, who cooked my meals for me for six long weeks when Jenny had to be away, remembered when she was tall and strong like her, and one night over the plates emptied of toad-in-the-hole and mash - with no teeth she always ate soft food - recalled wistfully the walks of a summer Sunday evening after chapel, a company of young people who cared not for tomorrow. To walk from the village to the next, and then back across the fields via a third, as the birds quietened in the hedges (but do the blackbirds ever cease their noisy startle before full dark?) and the bats came out, flitting across the early stars - it was company and fellowship, and privacy of a sort, for the fields and paths were then hedged with hawthorn or even the useful bullace. As she

Out of Reach

spoke, her memories ran into mine; for of just such a little flock, chattering among the hedges like September goldfinches, in just such surroundings, had Jenny and I only recently been part. (And now we were parents, who would all too soon have to worry what their daughter was getting up to!) Every time we now walk those four miles - our regular walk - something of Gwen's memories colours the horizon. But now the way of idle wandering is signposted, way-marked, and people with serious boots and bobble hats are to be seen in season. The bullace trees are still there, but few have have tasted the jam of that unforbidden fruit.

When we first knew the village there were still some women who had lived there all their lives for whom such walks had been fruitless. They never married; some, of course, must have seen their marriage prospects ruined by the carnage of the First World War. And some had a life of quiet, unsung service. Maisie the postlady, for example, was up every morning at six to bike over to the next village to pick up the post, cheerfully delivering it in all weathers (they use a car now, and our post is erratic, late and often soaked). After that, she went home to the long, low cottage by the river to cook her brother's breakfast when he came in off the farm, and to put her parents, one mob-capped, one imperiously moustached and be-capped, where they would catch the morning sun. Both were born before Gladstone ever formed a ministry. Nothing changed in that house and Lloyd George was still a name to invoke in political matters - 'He gave us a pension.' On Sundays, Maisie played the organ in the church, leading the singing of the hymns as her fingers found their way through the keys and stops. She taught both our children to play the piano. They sat beside her at the instrument, in the cool, twilit room that smelled of age and polish, the ornaments of a century around them, as many children before them had done. For Maisie loved children, and they

Out of Reach

loved her, though with the casual matter-of-factness of the growing. Even into her seventies she single-handedly ran a Sunday School, and tried to pass on to the young heathen something of the piety of the saints. I don't know whether it worked.

Sometimes marriage was cool. Old Aaron up the street was a gloomy type of chap. He and his wife lived in the same house, but were economical of speech with each other. Clearly, for them, 'for better for worse' had been unambiguously one-sided. Now they were old, and there was no softening of their stale hostility. But one Sunday, in the pub Aaron announced he had made his wife a present. We knew he was good with his hands, and had worked with wood when he was younger. There was a moment of astonished silence: he was clearly enjoying the attention.

'What is it, then?', someone asked, for Aaron clearly wanted his cue.

'I've med her a coffin.'

'But she en't dead.'

'Naow, not yit she en't, but when she is, I an't a-gooing to spend money on one for her now. Saved meself a bob or two.'

The story got around pretty fast. And it was true: he had made a beautiful coffin, which could be seen through the front window of their house standing upright for all the world as if waiting for its mummy. And it stood there for years, empty and inviting, to be glimpsed through the curtainless windows as we came past in summer, or, as the nights drew in, to be seen catching the flickering blue of Aaron's television. She had her story, I am sure, but we never heard it.

She never used the coffin, either. He did.

Out of Reach

Another old lady - why, when spinsters achieve a certain maturity do they acquire the right to be 'old ladies' rather than 'old women'? - was Tilly Bowyer, a very respectable straight-backed figure going about her mysterious business in her immaculate little house with the apple-pie garden. With age, she had become Somebody.

How do I recall Tilly? Seth and I were working at the front of the house one morning: we were taking to bits some wooden aircraft crates that I had bought, with the wood of which I intended to make a shed, and Seth was bent over a small anvil straightening the nails we saved. (Eventually, he filled a bucket, and I used them for ages. You did not waste good iron if you could avoid it, said Seth.) Tilly went past; greetings all round. As her determined little person went on up the hill, like a busy hen, Seth paused, and he looked ruminatively at her, while he rolled a fag.

'Dew yew knaow, bor, I remember the night she had her
Pants held up by nineteen safety pins.'

What could I say? Was he kidding me? I had no idea how
I was expected to react. But I remember Tilly for the safety pins if nothing else. (And, if there was some truth in the story surely Seth was not counting as he counted nails. . . .) And the only other memory of her - I cannot even remember where she went when she left, or when she died - is of a pitchy December night a few months later, with snittering rain; having to knock her up and being told 'Go Away! Go Away!'

'But, Miss Bowyer, Seth's died, and Mrs Seth says please can you come and lay him out.'

She came.

Out of Reach

Out of Reach

Chapter Seven

In the big house further along the river lived Colin, scientist, musician, organ builder, churchwarden, beekeeper. He was the only incomer like ourselves. It took a long time to get to know him, for we were wary of one to whom so many, by report, reacted so negatively. Indeed, the man who preached his funeral sermon said, in a voice that shook with love, that Colin was the rudest man he had ever met: the rudeness offended many people, to the point where they just wrote him off - and missed knowing one of the most kind and generous-hearted men it has been my lot to encounter. His rudeness was the rudeness of a clear mind, that sees to what it thinks is the heart of the problem and assumes you want to know; not the rudeness that comes from not thinking others matter, so much as the tactlessness that comes from thinking they see the world with the same directness and innocence as you do.

It was one still summer evening, and we were walking the dog: we had acquired him the winter before. In the distance, we could just discern the sound of a piano, and as we walked up the fen towards the village, the noise became notes, and the notes formed themselves into patterns, and the patterns became part of a Bach partita. We stood outside Colin's garden, letting the notes discuss among the trees. As the pattern drew to completeness, the swifts began their daredevil evening ritual, that communal hurtling towards the wall of the house only to turn, at the last second, like a skate's heel smooth on a bow-bend, with screams that ought to be of exhilaration. Their noise underlined the silence, their swoops the breathless panache of what we had just heard. As we stood there, Colin came out; and an uncomfortable, energetic, demanding friendship began.

Music was a first bond between us. Colin built organs as

other people make model aeroplanes, and quite soon he was running out of churches to put them in. Ever more ambitious in the specification and the technology, he collected pipes from dismantled instruments, panelling for cases from wherever he could get it, and his barn was full of a chaos of electronic mystery and bits that Bach would have recognised. To refuse one of Colin's organs was difficult, for his enthusiasm was loquacious; and, to be fair, they sounded better and better, until the last two he built came to be recognised as remarkably ingenious electronically and particularly well-suited to music of the high Baroque, which was his passion. Colin liked size: big pipes, big sound; and sometimes the installation and use of something that would faithfully reproduce the low frequencies of a 32-foot pipe in a smallish building caused flutterings of every kind. These were brushed aside, and Colin played yet more pyrotechnics on the new instrument to quieten opposition.

But he never reconciled the lady churchwarden, whose pew was right in front of the enormous mouth of the soundbox for the speaker that reproduced the 16-foot. Sitting behind her, we could see her glowering by the *Gloria*, by the first note of the *Sanctus* she was visibly shuddering. At Parochial Church Council meetings she made it clear, in her ladylike way, that she did not like the organ, and wanted it out. Stalemate. One Christmas came when Colin had put together a musical programme that excelled, even by his own high standards. The music before the service was magnificent, intoxicating; the liturgy continued with verve, even Peggy was clearly moved by the music. Then, in the middle of the sermon, a high-pitched whine set in, at the pitch which is impossible to ignore. Peggy waited until the Vicar had struggled through his sermon. We could see her glaring at Colin, as if to say, 'I knew that organ would I go wrong. Do something about it. Now.' And we could see Colin glaring back, determinedly sure that whatever was making this appalling, penetrating row, it was not his organ. The silent quarrel was far more gripping than the words of the sermon, alas. In the end, the noise continuing, as soon as Colin

Out of Reach

prepared to start playing the Creed, Peggy left her seat and went to the vestry, where she threw the main switch. The organ died, and a disconcert of voices straggled to the end of the great statement of belief. Nothing was said. For the noise continued. Right to the end of the unaccompanied last hymn. And beyond. It only went when old Mrs Camps left her pew, and slowly made her way out of church, taking her hearing aid with her. Relations between Peggy and Colin were better after that. Colin used the 16-foot less often, and Peggy stiffened only two or three times a service.

A second thing Colin and I shared was an interest in the past, particularly the local past. Where I listened to gossip, Colin dug, a natural archaeologist, with the crucial ability to make connections, think laterally, recognise the significance of the insignificant. His collection I lusted after: at his death, it disappeared, where I know not. Perhaps it was just thrown out, when the family moved away, for his children had no interest in his passions. Gradually the two of us, one approaching retirement, the other still unconsciously thinking summer's lease would have no end, came to do much together - a sort of more intellectual variant of the companionship Seth and I enjoyed. In our frequent disagreements, between ourselves, and on the Parochial Church Council, where we both were then serving, we came to respect each other's steel. We argued furiously, but we came to rely on each other for the helping hand, in the garden and wherever, which our wives might be too wise to lend.

And so I came to beekeeping. Colin had kept hives for years in the orchard that lay between us, and inevitably I was asked to help, first with the removal of honey, then with the regular inspections for queen cells and wax moth. Soon we were working them together, and I found myself interested enough to want some of my own. Beehives in the garden, I realise now, fitted the self-image to which I was half-

Out of Reach

consciously living up - the cottage surrounded by its produce, living as far as possible off the resources round it. (It was the time when I was reading Richard Jefferies and William Cobbett ...)

Colin found me some bees, from an old man who was giving them up. Their model polity arrived in the next January but one after the Bach partita, and they were installed under the big hawthorn that we came to love for the dark greenish honey its flowers produced for many springs (and its wood warmed us when it fell). I remember going to look at them with a sort of awe, and many questions at the back of my mind. For individual bees were just insects like any other, yet this great white thing gently snoring in the gathered dusk was like a great brain, that could remember, and plan, and predict, and remembered me vindictively for days after I had handled the bees, so that a veil was advisable when cutting the lawn. And while I was musing, to no particular consequence, about the nature of personality or the difficulties of keeping bees in hives woven of fennel stalks as Varro recommends in the *De Re Rustica*, the village watched, silently, to see what this odd young man would do next. For though most of the people who had grown up in the village had handled bees at some time, none now did, preferring the sweetness of white sugar to the bitterness of stings. They fully expected me to retire hurt, and soon. And I think they regarded my interest in the old crafts as strange: a lot of the old crafts that we romanticise (and do I?) were sheer hard work, and the people who were bound to them were glad to be shut of them as soon as they could be.

It was the same in so many areas. It is easy to slip (unconsciously) into romanticising the old ways of farming, but in fact many of the generations immediately previous to ours were glad to see them go. Nostalgia might bring elegiac regrets when there was no longer any danger of actually having to use the old ways, but for the countryman stayed on the land the twentieth century made life a great deal easier physically. It is very easy to feel nostalgic about pictures of a pair of Suffolks pulling a single-furrow plough but no

Out of Reach

ploughman would have willingly gone back to those miles of sheer effort in all weather that ploughing an acre with horses entailed. Nostalgia hides the start, before a winter dawn, to bait and groom the horses, to get them ready for the day, leading them through their patient work, taking them back to their stable at three, rubbing them down, watering them, feeding them. . . . Sugar-beet singling, chopping out with a hoe, or even hand-weeding the tiny plants, was back- and mind-breaking. Only twenty years ago men, women and children - every available hand - at the right time had to get down to that job, and children were kept off school to get it done. There may be something entrancing for the outsider, like me, who has just driven back from the town, in seeing a young girl, just becoming a woman, coming off the fen glowing with a day's sun, barefoot, with the black soil highlighting the curve of her calves (Parson Kilvert!). But there is nothing but an aching back for the young girl. And the man who had to clean acres of young wheat welcomed the coming of the chemical spray. Of course, the missionary vigour of youth led me to clash on this issue with many of the villagers. Like many of my generation, I had woken up to the dangers of chemical farming and the indiscriminate use of powerful, wide-spectrum sprays. I tried to persuade Young Albert, Albert's son, of the dangers - dangers that could be tangibly felt in the tightness of chest and the metallic taste in the mouth when he had been spraying against aphids. I got an inarticulate but unmistakably dusty answer. Yet the problem, I think, was not the argument, but the age-old one of the old resenting the insight of the young, the countryman resenting the supposed townie, the labourer resenting the book-learning of the scholar. Ironically, the very people with whom I tried to argue were themselves the first to complain of the lack of birds, of fish, of insects compared with the days of their youth.

I have a first edition of the *Observations in Natural History* by a scholar-vicar of an adjacent parish in the middle of last century. (It was Jenyns, the man who was to have gone on the *Beagle*, in fact, and suggested his friend Darwin go instead.)

Out of Reach

He inventories with indefatigable exactitude the insect, animal, and plant species to be found hereabouts. He records now unthinkable but well-attested things like the taking of a 112lb sturgeon at Ely in 1816 - mere curiosities, in fact; but he also records a range of birds and fish and butterflies several times greater than is now found, and some of the species of fish taken from the river here were taken in commercial quantities. I argued with people who remembered that richness, yet they would not make the connection that farming methods were largely to blame for the decline and that what destroyed one area of the web of life might have unknown consequences for ourselves, part of the same web. They trusted those who sold to them, they trusted the politicians, they trusted the man in the white coat, that mid-century badge of serious intent and integrity, the magician by another name.

I came to understand, in the end, a few of the reasons why chemical farming was so welcomed. It was certainly a great saver of time, and work, though it, and machinery, in the end caused there to be less jobs, and the capital cost of growing things probably stayed about the same. Short-term, the case was made. But there were deeper reasons as well. Seth, one hot day, sleeves rolled up on his whipcord arms, waistcoat open, was mixing up some brew in his bucket to spray on his young sprouts, which, like mine, were attacked by nasty grey aphids. He always added washing powder to whatever he sprayed: 'Makes it stick better, and yew gits lovely white spuds.' (The first part is true, but probably doesn't matter. . . .) As usual, I began pointing out that he would kill all the nice ladybirds as well as the nasty aphids, and if anything sprayed with the mixture could not (so it said on the bottle) be eaten for fourteen days afterwards, it must be pretty poisonous stuff. And so on, and so on - he had heard it all before, and did not bother to argue, just kept on mixing, slowly stirring the milky fluid round. Finally, as a clincher, I said, 'They did not use those things in the old days, they had good crops.'

He straightened up, and looked steadily at me with a seri-

Out of Reach

ousness that made me feel I had somehow touched an unsuspectedly raw spot.

'No, they di'n't use 'em. A powerful lot of crops failed. And people went hungry.'

He then carried on stirring. Seth was in no danger of going hungry, but he remembered when he was. The countryman of yesterday was always aware of the precariousness of the food supply; and many had known hunger. (Perhaps that is why the old ideal of feminine beauty was distinctly well-upholstered, for that showed her man was wealthy enough to feed her well: a promise, and proof, of plenty.)

The hunger, the hardship, the exploitation of the rural poor has been documented often enough: the prettiness of a Gainsborough painting of a thatched cottage, or the honeyed nostalgia of Goldsmith's Auburn got their comeuppance before the paint and the ink was dry from people like George Crabbe and William Cobbett. And country memories are retentive: I have spoken to men from the Isle of Ely who would refer to the Littleport riots of 1816 as if they, and the part the Bishop played in the hanging of the ringleaders, were still common talk. In the 1830s 'Captain Swing' had his eastern association; in the 1870s and later it was in Suffolk that the opposition to the unionisation of agricultural workers was most ruthless. When we came to the village, there were still old folk around who remembered the earlier years of the century with some bitterness. But memory is an odd thing. We remember with advantages: the tales of the hard years contained an element of pride - 'We survived'. They contained, more than we might be politically correct to allow, some (un?)conscious exaggeration. John from the Swaffham Prior relates how his grandfather used to berate him when, like any child, he didn't eat up the latest thing against which he had taken a fancy, 'When I wor a boy we wus glad to get what we could, dinner wor often just swedes.'

Out of Reach

And his mother (sensible woman, whom I knew as a little bustly body busy as her own hens in her farmyard) chipped in, 'Oh father, you do tell those children stories - you never went hungry in all your born days.'

Memory glamorises, in either direction - as I am sure, but cannot know, it is doing for me. It is, I think, a factor in the sort of remark I have heard more than once: 'Never been as well off as when I had twenty shilling a week and the old squire wor alive.' It is this that made one old lady overheard in the street say to her friend as the news was going round that the last scion of the squire's family - a grandnephew, I think - was going to come back to live in one of the houses the family still owned 'Won't it be lovely to have a squire again!': that was in about 1980. We all find some form of nostalgia irresistible, inevitable: just as Gillian Tindall has documented that in areas of London that have not seen fields and cows for a century and a half there are local old people who will talk of the pastoral idyll of their childhood there.

Sometimes, the more well-to-do might well recognise their responsibility to help, to improve the lot of the labouring classes - and make a bob or two out of it themselves. It was this impulse that led a vicar to build a new school-cum-chapel-of-ease in the village, to provide for the children who would otherwise have had to tramp two miles over to the school below the parish church. It was this that led one squire in Swaffham Prior village to build a reading room, so that the poor, newly literate as the consequences of the 1870 Education Act began to bear fruit, could improve themselves. It was the same squire who, concerned - with good reason - about the healthiness of the wells from which the village drew its water, built a little reservoir and an ornate little covered fountain to provide a clean supply. And, perhaps most telling of all, when the squire diverted the road from Cambridge so that it no longer went through his park, and built a causeway to carry it across a dry valley in the chalk, he planted the dry, stony sides of the causeway with lavender to provide work for the women of the village - filling lavender bags for sale, I imagine.

Out of Reach

But those works were largely for the main village, and did not impinge upon this hamlet. What did was the way one big farmer, who owned the land where the clunch had been mined for centuries, used to give his men work in the old quarries when times were slack on the farm. With picks they undermined the layers of hard chalk, and then brought the slabs down with crowbars. The blocks of stone thus won were dragged up the gentle slopes out of the quarry by horses, and down to barges waiting on the lode to be transported to Ely or Cambridge. But much of it was used locally, for road metal, or farm buildings, or houses. A load of clunch for local use would cost only a few pence. But more valuable than that was the work that farmer gave his men when the year was lean.

Nothing wasted: in the old cottage economy everything had a use. And it pleased us to think that the shades of those who had gone before would approve of our putting beehives in the garden. But, again, we did not know what we were taking on. Bees have a way of becoming very important - and unpredictable. Losing a swarm comes to feel like losing a fortune; the health of the bees can cause a sleepless night; and making sure they were content and well-supplied for winter had me tearing home from work in the middle of the day to fill up their feeder with syrup. They are also no respecters of situation, company or person.

One summer day Colin's wife was giving visitors elegant tea under the mulberry tree, and Colin, unable to sit and make small talk, was walking the lawnmower up and down to make sure the grass had not grown since he last cut it. Suddenly, to the consternation of the guests, he let go of the lawnmower, which continued on its single-minded way into a rose bed, and started taking his trousers off; but forgot to take off his shoes first. Now this sight was remarkable enough; it became even more intriguing when Colin, trousers

Out of Reach

now round his ankles, began to try and run, engaging the while in a sort of flagellation of his lower regions. Eve continued to pour tea and talked unconcerned, for she had seen this sort of thing before. Colin had been cutting in front of the hives, and a bee had crawled up trouser leg - probably with no nefarious intent, but an enclosed bee can do unpredictable things. And Colin had unwisely started to strip off right in the flightline of those hardworking and impatient ladies who had been out harvesting the flowers. Not unreasonably, they were offended.

Taking and hiving swarms is one of the great pleasures of the beekeeper - if all goes well. To empty the whole box of bees onto a white cloth, like the mix for Christmas pudding, and see the confused mass within seconds begin to order itself and move purposefully into the mouth of the hive you have prepared for them, is magical; but first you have to take the swarm, and bees consider not the beekeeper's convenience when engaged in seeking a new home.

The first swarm Colin had me take was right at the top of an old elder tree, in June, when the tree flowers. I am highly allergic to elder pollen. So, there I was, at the very top of a ladder on a hot day, swaying with the tree in the wind, attempting to hold a box over the swarm with one hand and smoke them so they would walk up into the box with the other. I was a very obvious object at the side of the garden, and quite soon a small knot of people had gathered to watch. And then, of course, I felt the grandmother of all sneezes coming... By the time I had been up and down the ladder half a dozen times to pick up the box, or the smoker, which I had dropped, I was beginning to feel that if Colin wanted these damn bees he could get them himself. But the next attempt seemed to go well, and the swarm did what it was supposed to do. I came cautiously down the ladder with the open end of the box towards the lawn, and placed it on the ground, leaving a small gap so stragglers and scouts would smell their queen and rejoin her in the box. Only, I had not got the queen. She was still in solitary majesty at the top of the elder tree, while her court was in a box on the ground. In that situation, the bees soon realise what has happened, and within minutes that box was empty and the loyal swarm was happily reunited with the queen at the top of the elder tree.

It took four goes to get that queen, by which time the knot of people had grown to a small crowd, and I was beginning to suspect they are not all there purely out of interest in bees. There were audible groans of disappointment when it became clear that this time I had got the queen: the show was over for the time being.

Bees and their handling were taken for granted in the old cottage economy: just one more way of making ends meet. The work the bees did was valuable even without the honey, as I noticed when my fruit and vegetable crops doubled the summer I put bees in the garden. Taking a swarm was literally child's play. Don told me of the times his father Stan, who used to keep many hives, would send him off to friends in the nearby villages with surplus swarms tied up in an old sack on the handlebars of his bike. Justin, who grew up with bees around, showed little fear of them, even, as we were working the hives, reaching his unprotected hand between the frames of comb to break off bits of honey-dripping brace comb, which we would have had to waste - and eating it there and then, sometimes brood and all. He took his first swarm, unaided, while I was away one summer: he would have been about ten. (The nonchalance with which he told me he had taken and hived them did not really hide the pride he clearly felt.) And I do confess to a certain envy: I remember my own childhood as far less interesting, far more cautious.

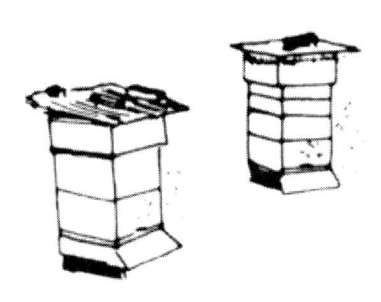

Chapter Eight

All communities have their dark side. It was easy, for Jenny especially, to see it, left alone in the dark, dank days of November with two toddlers and a large dog, surrounded by slurpy mud, in a house cold despite the good intentions of the boiler. But the winter passes: spring comes. The envies and jealousies could manifest themselves not as something vicious, but as practical jokes, or just sheer fun. All villages that are not quite dead have their jokers. Our village had its share, though now its changed population is perhaps too polite and too careful of its dignity to enjoy the type of humour that used to be.

Albert used to tell stories of how a horse and cart left standing outside one of the pubs might later take a good deal of finding if the owner stayed inside too long; nowadays, if a car was treated in the same way, the police would be called. And there was the classic prank played against the rag and bone man, who doubled as coal merchant. He liked his tipple. He left his horse and cart on the Green by the gate into a meadow. Two hours later, the horse was still there, patiently chewing the mysterious contents of its nosebag. It was still in the shafts. But now the cart was on the other side of the gate. Suddenly, the whole Green was dotted with people who had found they had nothing to do, while the rag and bone man, with a little too much Steward and Patteson Ely ale inside him, tried to get that horse to pull the cart through the gateway.

The men from the village down on the Cam three miles away had for generations been 'That Upware Lot', and there was little love lost between the two communities. I never found out why - though I did find out that a one of their farmers or smallholders would shoot the dog of a man from

Out of Reach

our village if it strayed onto his land - and take him to court for poaching given half a chance. But most of the year the two villages rubbed along together, and by our time the old rancours existed only in the memories of the older folk, who had lost the physical power to do much about them, But many told me of how until just before the War the riverbank men would come up along the river in a body at the time of the annual fair, and get their annual haircut in one of the booths. They would then fill themselves up in the beer tent. And then the men of the two villages would have an almighty bout of fisticuffs, which ended up with the losers being pitched into the river. The constable, whose duty it was to make sure, according to the proclamation that opened the fair, that 'all evilly disposed persons should remove themselves on pain of imprisonment', could do nothing. And, as a local man, perhaps regretted that his uniform prevented his joining in the annual ritual.

The only relic in our time of the days the old men remembered as heroic was the tug of war between teams from the two villages, held across the river. The teams trained for months, getting to the point where they could uproot decent sized trees. And then, with much straining and sweating, one side pulled the other one slowly but steadily into the river. And bought them a drink afterwards.

All part of the yearly routine of the village, and the parish, as it had been for centuries, starting at the turn of the year with the Plough Monday customs that lasted into the 1960s, the Rogationtide services and fair, and going through to the horkey, the harvest supper that used to be given by the farmer to the team of reapers who had mowed his fields. (That went long ago,)

Plough Monday - the Monday after Twelfth Night - cannot, in the old days, have been the time when, as some say, the major ploughing of the year was started. (Thomas Tusser, indeed, suggests most of the ploughing should be done in October and November.) For if that work was not done before Christmas, you could probably forget about having the land dry enough to plough and then work to a tilth fit for planting in the spring. The day marks, instead, an ancient custom of obscure origin: it may be that favourite of anthropologists, a fertility custom, or it may have arisen in the later mediaeval centuries simply as a means of raising funds - just as church ales did. Other bits of these ancient customs survived until recently - for example, the blessing of the plough. In some parishes a plough was kept in the parish church itself for the use of the poor. In this parish, several men we knew recalled how in the 1930s on Plough Monday the children, with blackened faces, carried a plough round the village to the more well-to-do houses. There was the understood threat to plough up the doorstep of any who refused to give money, and as they went the children sang

> A sifting of chaff, a bottle of hay
>   See the poor crows go carrying away,
> Squeak by squeak they wag their tails.
>   Hi nonney! Hi nonney!

The 'Hi' was shouted as loud as they could yell. One farmer would make them come forward singly and to each child he would give a sixpence - a goodly gift. Once they had grasped it firmly, they would turn and run as hard as they could with the farmer's huge whip - I have one myself - cracking at their heels as he laughed at them. (One can imagine the number of social workers who would descend on that innocent scene nowadays!)

Come spring and the first of May, and the girls made May dollies - until about 1960 or so. They took the prettily dressed dolls round the houses, showing them to people: but, unusually (the custom is known from elsewhere), in this parish the acceptance of money was forbidden.

Come harvest, and old Albert made a bunch of ears of the new wheat and hung it on a nail outside his door. 'That's my sample', he said, and it stayed there until the winds of winter greyed its gold. But (did he know it?) it was no such thing, was much, much older a custom.

These forgotten customs touch a stratum of country life

that is rapidly becoming irrecoverable, except as an antiquarian curiosity - like Morris dancing. (And where once no woman, by custom reaching back five hundred years to the courtly origins of the dance, would ever have wanted to be allowed in the dancing patterns, I now see women taking part. . . .) What is left is the games of children, the odd saying, the strange superstition. 'Yew walk round our Church seven times the Devil will appear.' There were folk who would not have elder-wood - the witch wood, the tree on which Judas hanged himself - in the house. They would not burn its close-grained, hard wood. And yet there was a foul-smelling ointment made of it called 'Zambuk' (elder's Latin name is *sambuca*) which Mrs Seth smeared daily on the sores on her legs. The ancient reverence for the hawthorn, the May tree, showed itself in the way Phil exclaimed, on seeing a vase in which sprays of the delicate flowers of hawthorn were included, 'Yew'll never thrive with May in the house; tek that out!'.

Animals had their force too. 'An 'orse with four white stockings, that en't no good.' 'Yew sh'd spit and wish when yew see a piebald 'orse - but don't yew tell anyone what yew did wish.' Or hares: I once casually remarked to Mrs Seth that as I drove back from Cambridge that day I had seen a hare running through the village. Her reaction was one of obvious horror: 'That's calling for someone.'

For the first time - I have met it many times since - I had stubbed my toes on the belief that hares were somehow supernatural in their affiliations. Running through a village, they foretold a death, or a fire, or some other disaster. There were still folk about, I found, who would tell you that their uncle, or their grandmother - never they themselves - had believed that hares were really witches. (They said it in such a shifty way that you could see they themselves were not sure they were not.) 'hose old Sallies (the Cambridgeshire name for a hare) ut there, there's some dew say they ent othing else but witches. . . .' (I wonder if this was why some people did not relish hare all that much as a dish.) For Mrs Seth, it was much clearer: she dreaded the loss of Seth, and my mention of the hare brought that dread out of where she had tried to bury it.

Soon after we had begun to grow vegetables, I called in the shop one morning on the way to work and happened to remark to Toby that I wanted to get some peas in that evening. 'So yew like to plant with the moon, then?' he asked - and I was totally nonplussed. But soon I found out what he meant. I was given the advice in all seriousness by several men that when planting for seed or fruit - like peas, or beans - you should plant with the waxing of the moon; and when planting for roots, plant with its wane. To one who had only thought of the moon in so far as its phase affected the tides and the placing of a nightline on a Lancashire beach, this was news indeed. The temptation to dismiss the advice as mere superstition was tempered by the respect I had come to have for Toby, and Ben, and Ray - all of whom knew the ways of plants. I was realising that growing things was an art, not a science. And I was aware that something of immeasurable antiquity had been passed on.

Rogationtide: the year had warmed at last, and the local wisdom seemed to be true: 'It's always good weather for the Fair.' Until 'They' changed the date to the Spring Bank Holiday, it usually was. From the beginning of the thirteenth century, the fair had always happened in those days of early summer. Once a big, an international, affair, even a century ago it was declining from what it had been, though it was still an important horse fair. In 1904, 'Smaller than ever,' the newspapers report, 'trading in horses constituted practically the only business part of it, and the animals were in short supply.'

Out of Reach

But even today its ghost is still opened with great ceremony by the civic dignitaries of Cambridge, who own the right of market and the right to the dues and fines from a court of pie powder duly proclaimed. Pennies were thrown to crowds lining the route in the villages on the road from Cambridge, and before motor transport the Burgesses and the Mayor would have spent a day or so on the journey, with a consequent drain on their largesse. It was, when we came to the village, a mere fun fair, like so many of the old fairs. The only genuine trader was Jack Reynolds, 'The Rock King', who lived in Rockafella House in Cambridge, and sold violent-coloured rock with the village name all through it, and sticky fudge and other sweets. The village beer tent came out each year - it still does: the ex-army olive green that must go back to the years of Hitler's war still keeps out the sun from the smell of beer and trampled grass. An enterprising committee for a time revived something of the sale of horses and tack; they brought to it a pageant, plays and mumming, cake and plant stalls, and the pretty nostalgia of the schoolchildren, unfamiliarly neat and scarved, dancing round a portable maypole. (I remember, when I served as one of the School Managers, the formal proposal, and seconding, each year, of a motion to grant the children a day's holiday for the Fair.)

After Evensong on the Sunday before the fair, an unfamiliarly large congregation, embarrassed in suits grown tight, hair brilliantined flat, would troop out of church behind the Vicar and walk round the village asking a blessing on the crops. (Once they would have walked the boundaries, I think.) Down on the Hythe, where now the sewage works eructates, we solemnly blessed the cow parsley ('Queen Anne's Lace', the lovelier name) which grew straight and tall.

(The first time we went was another of those startling elisions: myself in cassock and surplice - they had a job to find one small enough - Uncle Alec's Church of Englandy voice intoning the Collect as the wind from the Lakeland fells fluttered the pages of the Prayer Book. 'I will lift up mine eyes unto the hills' rang through my head, as the lone and level fen stretched into the setting sun.)

Out of Reach

The village *en fête*, the first time we saw it. Faces unfamiliar above shirts with collars. Faces suggestive of people we know, with teeth in, with make-up. Instead of the everyday flat caps, trilbies - or, at least, a clean flat cap. Toby in his uniform as special constable, only just getting into it after all those expansive years: a Donald McGill policeman. Families reunited - everyone comes back for this yearly fair, everyone (except the slovens) tidies up the village, cuts the hedges, chops the nettles, whitewashes the walls, cleans the windows 'for when the Mayor comes'. (People think I am painting my wall for the same reason.) Not yet the piped music of later years - just the hubbub of expectancy. On the Green, next to the war memorial, the Silver Band from the next big village, in blue uniforms and peaked hats, very smart, their instruments sparkling in the May sun as the wind stirs the sheets of music clipped to them. The Band is of all ages, from striplings barely able to cope with a cornet to solid citizens, overflowing chairs too small for them, holding tubas and euphoniums. Their chairs slowly slant sideways into the soft earth while they wait. The schoolchildren have, by tradition, a holiday, and are making no more nuisance of themselves than usual.

The procession arrives, splendid in scarlet and furs, and the top-hatted Sergeant at Mace proclaims the right of those he serves to summary jurisdiction over a band of traders who have not gathered here today, and who came only in the memory of the oldest folk present - Maisie's father in his long wind-along wheelchair with its leatherette rain cover, or Kate, unfamiliar in a blue straw hat the rotundities of which have faded with years of storage. And new-minted pennies are cast into the crowd, as they have been for seven hundred years, and children scramble for them in the dust. The Silver Band strikes up with 'God Save the Queen', and everybody feels very solemn, very English. Then as the procession moves off, to proclaim the same court of pie powder at the deserted stone among the meadowsweet on

Out of Reach

the Hythe where once the horses were auctioned, and then to enjoy a meal in the old schoolroom, the Silver Band begins its performance. 'Oh, Listen to the Band' they begin with. . . .

And suddenly, my hand is in my grandmother's on the North Pier at Blackpool - the same hand from which splintersof that same pier have just been extracted with a hot kaolinpoultice - as we walk down to the glass-walled sun lounge to listen to Toni and his orchestra. You can see the sea between the planks, and I am a little afraid of that. (My grandmother is wearing a fox fur, and the head with its glass eyes dangles above mine: I am a little afraid of that too, especially when she bends down to me.) And Toni's ,' audience is all elderly ladies, for (though I do not know it) | most of the men are engaged in war work.

The two moments elide: the Silver Band sits above the remembered sea of long before, playing 'Poet and Peasant', and popular classics - though they do not rise to the bits of Mozart, and Spohr, and Beethoven, and the easier Wagner, with which Toni regaled those who had been washed up on that shore of England (Toni wore white tie and tails). Memory reaches further and further back to the things I never knew I knew.

Fairs and raree shows: perennial enjoyment.

> A live cat with wings resembling those of a duckling is now being exhibited in the neighbourhood by Mr David Badcock of the Ship Inn. The cat, which is a year old, did not until recently expose such a remarkable freak of nature, but being somewhat roughly handled spread out its wings. The owner charges the sum of 2d for callers inthe daytime to see such a strange being and has commenced taking it round the neighbouring villages in the evenings to exhibit.
> (*Independent Press*, 3 August 1894).

Out of Reach

The coming of the railways killed a lot of the fair's trade. Wilf could recall the village full of big, slow Suffolks and agile Welsh ponies, some still unbroken, that over several weeks had been driven there for sale: the village loud with the noise of horses being trotted up and down to show their paces, the whinnying of stallions, the chatter of different accents. The pubs full of the honest and the dishonest, the sellers of quack salves (I found boxes of them in our old shed) made of elder bark and even worse-smelling things, the sellers of bad leatherwork as well as good, the pickpockets, the visiting ladies from the town. For this was the high point of the rural year, the time of year that marked the easy season, when the worst of the spring land work was done, and only the haysel punctuated the warm months up to the beginning of the rye, and then barley, and then wheat harvest. This was the time which reminded old men to tell us of how, as children, they swam in the river, and fished, and climbed trees, and lay young and easy under the apple boughs, about the lilting house and happy as the grass was green.

Our children, too, followed the village pleasures of those who had gone before them. They made rafts out of old planks and oil drums, and played on the river as children must have done for centuries. In a plastic dinghy, a later gift, they made a voyage through the jungle of overhanging meadowsweet and nettles up the river a good mile to the source of the Orinoco. They were undoubtedly in some sort of danger - about as much as when they were high in their tree house in the crown of a grown-out pollard willow. But we let them, as we had ourselves been allowed, in other trees and other waters, and as all the children in the village had been allowed when their jobs were done. The fear culture of the last decades had not yet spread its poison; and we trusted, as we could, the goodwill, and the responsibility, of others.

Once, but before our time, early summer had been the

Out of Reach

season for the women's cricket team, which played in a meadow near the village, and travelled to away matches in a barge pulled along the river by their men. This was the season when large groups formed to bathe in the river, and the younger men ran Hare and Hounds in the fen. Once there was a sports club, with football and cricket teams, and regular fixtures. Its notice board, brown paint peeling, the white lettering still legible, is there yet. I have seen photographs of the teams of those days, men I knew as bent with the wind of years strong and tall, posing for posterity with the pride of youth.

The bathing place is still discernible: the remains of where the diving board stood are still there. We used it, once, one very hot day, with Jenny holding Antonia, and me dunking Justin. The dog did not like us doing any of this, and came in too, to try to get us out. I can still feel the luxurious slipperiness of the mud between my toes, and the curious silkiness of that water, full of life, on a skin that had known only the bite of sea water or the sterile stink of chlorinated. No-one swims now.

The big horses sold at the fair were far too dear, and needed too much feed, for the small men in the village to own one. Their ploughing, and carting, had to be done by the little ponies they bought at the fair: still called ''orsses', but undeniably ponies. Occasionally a donkey would be used by the poorer - far more often, and recently, than one might think, the familiar beast of peasant Italy and Greece worked this land. I have a photograph of my house with the tenant holding his donkey - taken around 1910, I guess. The old villagers would have looked on mystified at the present population of riding ponies in the village; an animal was for work, not play; and if it did not pay its way, off to the knacker's with it. Some did hold their beasts in a sort of affection, it is true, and it showed in odd ways. I know where, to this day, in a

Out of Reach

forgotten shed full of old junk that has not been shifted in thirty years to my knowledge, the father of the present farmer hung up the skin of a much-loved Suffolk Punch in the rafters. It is there still, moth-eaten but recognisable, and keeps some of the bird droppings off he Jacobean door that has been chucked in the back of a 1930s Leyland truck with flat tyres and a broken headlight. The truck was his first, and the horse almost his last. The Jacobean door has been around for a bit longer.

Seth had his ponies from time to time, and used to take them to Cambridge and do small commissions for people at threepence a go - pick up a parcel here, get some supplies there, perhaps give someone a lift. He had one that clearly stood out from the rest, a 'gibbun' horse he called it, mystifying me into thinking this was a special and desirable breed, until I realised he meant it jibbed a lot. He described the various ways of sorting the beast out - some, involving nettles and brambles, not to be approved of by animal lovers. But apparently the creature would just stop, for no reason, and refuse to move. 'And so I gets down, and I picks up a stone, and lifts its near fore, and taps it three times. And dew yew knaow, that old 'orse wor just waiting for that, and he just goo like the wind all the way home.' That, evidently, was the usual treatment. I heard the story several times.

Now, what I cannot understand is why my mind's eye has been able so convincingly to contextualise what I have never seen, or even heard fully described. I can see the horse, and the cart, on the curve of the road - I know it well - by the river in the next parish, the road dusty (for this is a summer before the tarring of roads), and the signpost is three feet higher than it is now for ease of reading by persons on horseback. I can see Seth, and the horse - a grey - and the incident. It is as sharp as if I were there. Yet he gave me none of these details, and I have not consciously created them: they just appeared in the mind, a fully rounded, historically detailed vignette. In a similar way, through the eyes of old men, I can glimpse, sharply, a time when their wives were young and beautiful. How?

Chapter Nine

The village, like others in the neighbourhood, grew in the first place because the resources of the fen were on its doorstep. Its folk for centuries looked to the levels as folk in coastal villages looked to the sea: as a place whence came work and sustenance and the sinews of life. And the analogy with a coastal village is close. For dry - too dry, some say - as the fen now is, it is a landscape formed by water, whose flatness - especially when scarves of low fog mask it - can look like the interminable shores of some vast sea. Water determines the rhythm of the ditches that plot its mass into articulation and control; water is the suppressed but never quite banished enemy. Long ago, the rising of the water-table killed the wildwood of oak, and beech, and pine and yew, and when the trunks fell a blanket of peat grew to cover their long sleep. The marsh grew in places to a prodigious depth, and provided fuel, and summer grazing, and winter fowling for generations upon generations: far from being waste, it was a land fully used by man. The river, three miles distant as the crow flies, and its once meandering tributaries, have had a huge effect on the way the fen-edge villages developed, and still, to some extent, think. Even for the generation that preceded us, the water and the river affected a large part of their lives.

Once upon a time - I do not remember it - a couple of hundred people had lived down the drained fen, in scattered houses, or odd groups, cut off in winter. They had had their own Post Office, which survived into my time, long after all trace of the dispersed settlement had gone, and the foundations of the houses had been ploughed out. People whom we knew had been brought up in those cottages in the fen, and remembered with no great pleasure their winter isolation. For

Out of Reach

with the coming of the wet weather, effectively, their chances of getting out of the fen with any ease disappeared until the waters receded and the land began to dry with the winds of March. In winter the roads and tracks became black mud, deep up to a horse's belly, and quite impossible for wheeled traffic. You laid in your supplies for the winter in good time; and you learnt to be able to manage without the services of doctor or clergyman. . . .

We have always known the road down the fen as a made road, with tarmac. Those hard roads, put in during the Second World War by the War Agricultural Committee, are now twisted and heaved and cracked by the wasting of the drained peat beneath. Many could remember the fen roads before the War as simple tracks. In 1904 a visitor passing through described it as 'almost impassable', 'alternating between so many inches of dust in summer and so many inches of mud in winter', an 'awful quagmire'. Yet on the riverbank was a pub, and 'dotted about were little farmhouses...there were sounds of abundance of cattle'. There was 'a ferry boat and drawboat' at the Cam, and a 'little Wesleyan chapel, and another public house'.

At its last right angle round the corner of a field the road swings to follow the line of the flood-bank, now high above it on the left. Beyond the flood-bank lie the washes. In summer, the slow stream of the Cam meanders politely through them, and on the wide plain on each side cows have long grazed: the lowland English landscape of the art gallery. The wetter places, curving now nearer, now further from the river, preserve a memory of where once the riverbed had run, and there once-pollarded willows lean still, sloped by the wind. Reeds grow to make a haunt where snipe, and coots, and mallard, and geese go about their summer business. Over the spongy ground the ear will in season often catch the sudden 'burrr' of a snipe as it power-dives in its display flight. By the water, the flash of a kingfisher, perhaps. A busy landscape, where other people go about their affairs, and a man intrudes. But in winter, the river can take back its own, as one day it will for good. Held back by the sluice at Denver, the

Out of Reach

waters coming down from the clay lands of Bedfordshire and the last spurs of the Chilterns pond back, flooding the washes for mile after mile after mile. Then the migrants come (in less numbers than they used to) on the easterly winds of early winter, the swans - whooper, Bewick's and mute - the geese, great skeins of them pulsing their way through the sky from the Baltic, from Russia, from the brief summers of the rim of the world. Some of them used to fall to the waiting guns, and the winter flights fed many a family in its lonely home as the wind scoured the land outside and raised breaking waves on the face of the flood. There were still men around, men whose hard hands I have shaken and whose stories I have half-believed, who waited for the coming of the winter birds as the Plains Indians waited for the migration of the bison. A single shot was no use to them. They remembered punt- and sledge-gunning for the swans and the duck. No nonsense about sport: this was serious business, which stocked the market stalls of Bury and Cambridge, and places even further off, and put money in the pocket of a man who had children to feed.

The gun-punt was simply a killing machine. Tarred, double-ended, and basically rather like a Norfolk coast flattie, its sole purpose was to carry a gun and a man - just: the man lying prone behind the gun, which could be eight feet or more in length, weigh over a hundredweight, and have a bore of two inches. Many guns were muzzle-loaded with black powder and wadding of oakum or even grass; several of the bigger ones could fire a pound of No 2 shot at a time. You chose a calm day, when the water was smooth; and you lay in the punt, its draught no more than three inches, and moved it gently through the shallow water with two short 'stalking sticks' over the low side. Stealthily, so slowly, you lined yourself up, downwind, on a flock of duck, or geese, or swans taking their ease on the water - preferably getting between them and any strong light. Any incautious movement now, or breaking of the low silhouette of man and punt and gun, would send them wheeling off into the sky. Wait for them to bunch. Then fire. The recoil would send you several feet back

Out of Reach

in the water - hence the need for the boat to be double-ended. (You kept your shoulder out of the way of the padded butt - let the movement of the gun be under the shoulder.) And, when the cloud of smoke cleared, there would be the birds, as many as a couple of dozen at a time, dead on the water ahead.

In a great frost, when the thin birds stand disconsolate on the ice that starves them, the punt-gun would be mounted on a sledge, behind a screen of reeds. The older sledges were mounted on four marrow bones - people still used bone skates in the last century. The gunner, kneeling behind the reed screen, pushed the contraption along with an iron-tipped spike in each hand. Firing sent man and gun and sledge many yards across the ice.

Barbarous? Different times, different ways: but the same need to fill a belly and keep a family, to make a living from what the land offered at the different seasons. Ben Jonson mentions the sending of water-birds from the fens to London tables - including ones we would not think worth the plucking, like godwit. Walking on the washes one summer, we came across hard evidence of how the fowlers had worked. A shallow pond, nearly covered over with reeds, betrayed by its star shape that it was man-made. An old decoy, that once upon a time would have netted hundreds of birds a season for its owner. There are many of them in the fens, and where the fens have been drained and they have been ploughed out, they have sometimes given their name to the field or the farm: Decoy Farm is common enough.

The principle is ingenious. Each arm, or 'pipe', of the star of water curved, and narrowed, until it could be covered over with netting - getting lower and narrower the nearer the end. Along each side of the pipe, a yard or so back, were a number of overlapping wattle screens. Now, duck are inquisitive creatures, and they will tend to investigate anything of interest if they feel secure. They also have a hatred of foxes - not unreasonably, since foxes will sneak up on a duck sleeping on the bank and grab it. So, the fowler had a dog as small and foxy looking as he could find - though this was not essential. The

Out of Reach

dog was trained to trot away from the pond along the gap between screens and water, and then turn and disappear for an instant behind a screen. And then again. The fowler chose a pipe into which the wind was blowing - otherwise the duck might smell the man - and set his dog to work. The duck would kick up a fearful racket, and charge the retreating figure of the dog. And further, and further, into the pipe, round the bend, below the net - then the man stands up and shows himself. The duck rush headlong to the end of the narrowing channel, into the narrow tube of the trammel net, where they pile up on top of each other in their panic. A quick pull with a cord, and the trap closes. One by one they are taken, their necks broken with a flick of the wrist, and the fowler has earned his keep. A technique that was harvesting the myriad waterfowl in this wet land long before the first Elizabeth is now all but forgotten. I have talked with men who said they had done it, but the catches, compared with those made before the draining of the land, were small.

> Beasts, urg'd by us, their Fellow Beasts pursue,
> And learn of Man each other to undo.

The dog, I doubt not, liked its work, and could not bother its head about a moral issue. Indeed, I have seen the pleasure in my own dog's eyes and dropped ears as he retrieved a shot bird and gave it into my hand. I have seen him old, arthritic, unable to follow the gun, look up and wag his tail with a look into my eyes that even now, long in memory, breaks my heart, when I took the gun off its nail to go out for a rabbit. In his youth he loved to 'trace the mazes of the circling hare', and even caught a young one once - no mean feat for a big-boned labrador. That working together of man and dog is a small miracle, that those who only know a dog as a pet, or companion, can never, I think, understand. Or the ache when it is there no longer.

Out of Reach

Sometimes the river got above itself. Sometimes even the washes filled to the brim. Old Albert told me of winters when volunteers from the fen villages worked day and night to strengthen the flood-banks with willow faggots and sandbags against the tide of waters swelled by snow melt and rain. Their own homes, their own fields, were at risk. The waves driven by a gale might not break their force on the willow bundles stacked on the banks, and the banks might well burst, as they had before, flooding the fields many feet below them, and drowning the stock. Then the land took weeks to be pumped dry and workable again.

I have never seen flooding on that scale, though many in this part remembered the breaches of the winters of 1947 and 1953. But I can imagine what the effect on the wild things must have been like. Even after a very wet spell lasting only a few days, when the washes drain out after flooding, round every little higher patch of ground is a tidemark of twigs, and bits of reed, leaves, and plants, berries, and dead things - beetles, worms, moles. Rich pickings for the birds, who may well have gone hungry while the waters covered the face of the land. The winter army of plovers, in their smart white waistcoats, their crests erect, stand at watchful attention, then double neatly to pick up in the flotsam a titbit that has caught their eye. The starlings - and winter brings great flocks of them - squabble as only starlings can over a harvest of the waters that will feed them all, and more. Further out a heron may stalk. The drowned-out worms fatten plover, starling, and snipe alike, and rooks soon find this common table. Foxes, at night, pick their way along these tidemarks, for they will eat worms and beetles with relish - and there is always the chance of something bigger being washed up. Rabbits and hares can both swim pretty well - indeed, I have seen a chased rabbit take to the water by choice and swim faster than a man in gumboots can wade. But even they can be trapped by the water, and find their strength fail them before they reach drier ground.

'Green Christmas, full churchyard', they say, and many a time a green Christmas heralds a wet winter. The graveyards of some of the fen villages were very little above the water-table, and by February, as it rose, a six-foot grave might have a couple of feet of water in it. I have been told of the practical custom of strewing fresh reeds, or, if the grass was beginning to grow, fresh grass scythings, in the grave just before the burial, so that the surface of the water would be covered. But the coffin would not have floated away to the tidemark with all that earth on it. ...

The fen is tamed now, we are told, and the lower water-tables no longer float tools and bottles in cellars and new-christen the dead. Since the cutting in the 1960s of the Cut-Off Channel right round the basin of the fens to catch the water of the rivers on the high land, the surplus water has gone direct to the sluice at Denver, and no longer finds its way, as once it did, through the maze of channels and slow streams to the Great Ouse. The pumps can cope with vast volumes of water, and in most years the ecologist and the conservationist will look at the fen and say the Internal Drainage Board is pumping it too dry for its good. Perhaps. Year by year the peat shrinks, and blows away, and the surface of the land gets further and further below the level of the rivers. If ever those banks burst.... Every year there is a new patch of sodden ground where the water has seeped through the bed of puddled clay with which generations of men's sweat has lined the straight canals, every year the land sinks that little bit more, and eastern England tilts that little bit more into the sea. One day the sluice and the banks will not hold against a great surge of the sea; one day the birds will feast on the tideline that will mark where once the drained land began. *Naturam expellas furca*. . . .

Out of Reach

A wet winter to flood the washes and a great frost to freeze them has been rare in recent years, but we have seen the ice glow with the last level rays of the sun as the growling skate flashes in the turn. To skate alone, with even pace, into the gathering dusk across ice that seems limitless - to pause, and hear the silence - yes, we have been lucky. But a really hard frost, a frost that set in, used to be no joy to the men and women who worked the land, no joy to the animals. Many recalled cruel winters when, because of the frost, there was no work to be had on the farms, and men, not wanted, had to make ends meet as best they could. In a hard frost I have shot birds so thin that their breast-bones stood out like keels, and the toll taken of the kingfishers by frozen water can be terrible. Even I have known frosts so intense that the hens could hardly feed before their mash froze, when a wild duck, in a frenzy of starvation, would come and eat from the hand that on other occasions had held a gun. The black ribbons of the salted road could so easily in moonlight and snow deceive the desperate water-birds into thinking that here at last was open water and a chance of food. And, weakened as they were, uncomprehending, I have known them sit on the road that should be water to be flattened by the traffic.

Then, in summer, the fen was full of insects that bit and buzzed and crawled and got in eyes and ears. Worst of all were the flies, ranging from little houseflies through the iridescent 'greenbottles' whose maggots will kill an undipped lamb in three days, to the speedy, heavyweight bluebottles. It is difficult, now, to recall the torment they were. They were everywhere. Leave the windows open in the sun, and in they poured. On windows, on paintwork, on the backs of books, a pox of fly specks. Leave food uncovered, and the creatures found it in an instant, pausing and rubbing their hands over it. They fell into cooking pans; they crawled over skin; they made specks all over windows, and lightbulbs, and lamp-

Out of Reach

shades. They nearly drove us frantic. Their hum was the constant noise of quiet summer. We went to church, and found that the flagon for the communion wine had a muslin cover over it, and had had ever since one Sunday the Vicar had found a pickled fly in the consecrated Sacrament. The older folk smiled at our distress, for to them this was simply the way things were. They kept their curtains half closed, and used glass bell-jars baited with sugar water to catch them as their forebears had before them. But the flies to us were terrible, and down the fen the air was a soup of gnats and mosquitoes. There were horse flies too, and there is a limit to how often one can admire their beautiful green eyes with any enthusiasm.

Hence, perhaps, the welcome countryfolk have for the martins, and the swifts, and the bats who each year came to share the house with us; and our welcome for the spiders who every autumn find their way to winter quarters. A child quoted her mother at us: 'If you want to live and thrive, Let the spider walk alive.' Each bat eats three thousand insects per night: more power to its elbow. So, one day, when I was up a ladder cementing up a bad gap between the slates and the brick of the roof gable, Jenny suddenly said, 'The swifts can't get in.' No more they could: they were wheeling near me in my temporary eyrie in some desperation. And so, hardly repining, I took out the cement I had just smoothed in. ('It'll wait.') We began to look forward to each year to the coming of the swallows and swifts and martins. They are regular: round here the swallows arrive around 23 April, and the swifts depart on or about 8 August. (The dates are very close to Gilbert White's.)

The birds became one of the enduring pleasures - hearing the martins gurgling to their brood outside our bedroom window in the early morning, or sitting watching the swifts in the evening - until, suddenly, the air is no longer full of the swing of swifts but with the angular flight of bats. Swifts go higher as the dark rises from the earth on a still evening, wheeling in the last of the light over the banks of trees or orchards where thermals deliver them their dinner. Their

Out of Reach

languid, predatory patrolling continues, until, stirred by a single scream, they all begin their madcap triumphal speedway (their wings now faster than the eye can easily see as they put on speed). Woe betide the late, peaceable martin, grazing on the fields of air, that gets in the way: a corvette charged by a phalanx of destroyers. I have seen them tumble out of the sky before recovering themselves.

The buzz of summer flies, the wind under the door in winter - our house sang the same songs as all the others that looked out over the fen. Even so, the materials of which it had been built, like those of many of its period, showed how the immemorial dependence on what the marsh and the hill could provide was weakening. They came from far away as well as from the hill behind us: industrialisation and cheap bulk transport changed for ever the old exclusive reliance on local materials. But there was still a lot of evidence of how things used to be done, in other older houses, in garden sheds and walls, and in the way the older people still used techniques their fathers had taught them. And invented new ones.

Down the fen Harold Sennett had bought himself a second-hand baler, one of the first that compressed the straw into rectangular bales bound with twine. His farm was open to every wind of heaven, and the winter gales that drifted the thin snow into the ditches and the summer dust storms that put black banks of blown peat across the roads roamed uninterrupted across his flat acres. There was a need for a shed, or a barn, or something, just to shelter equipment and men when they took a rest, but for years he just put up with it. Then the baler came: and suddenly, Harold realized, years before trendy eco-building, that bales could be made into very good building material. Build them up like huge bricks, a few sheets of corrugated iron ('tin') on some bits of wood for a roof, and you had a warm and weathertight shed. It stood for years. I have sheltered in it many times, and noted

Out of Reach

that it soon became a sort of little home. Chairs appeared; a small stove to brew up; and there was evidence that Harold's son found it a useful place to do his courting. The place was warm and cosy for years, until the tireless searchings of the rats, making their runs through the straw walls, brought them down in dust.

Harold Sennett was only doing what generations of people had done before him: intelligently using what was to hand. The wall along the side of our garden, flanking had been the dock where the barges used to unload, looked conventional enough: roughcast, with a tile top. But when the tiles began to fall off, and the weather got in, it soon became clear the wall - some century or so old, as far as I could find out - was simply clay bats with quoins of clunch. The bats were made simply by digging the blue-grey gault clay - in fact any clay would do - and puddling it with chopped straw in a pond made for the purpose. The straw and the broken clay were heaped up, and liberal quantities of water and salt added. Then a horse was tied to a post in the middle, and driven round and round and round. When the mess had been homogenised into something slimier and stickier than stiff porridge, it was moulded into blocks - about eighteen inches by six by nine - and allowed to dry. A few days in the summer sun and the blocks were hard, capable of carrying a surprising load if bedded well with lime mortar. At one time, in a countryside where wood is scarce, most houses were built of such material: indeed, the ponds by many ancient houses are simply the ponds where the daub was puddled for the bats or for plastering onto the woven hazel or willow between timber frames. When it has been standing for years and has been colour-washed, you cannot tell it is simply mud. (Until you hear the rats scuttling through their runs in the walls, as in Harold Sennett's shed.) It will stand for hundreds of years if you keep the rain out, yet keep it slightly damp: the addition of salt stopped any chance of the walls freezing and then crumbling. It was a curious feeling to see our garden wall crumble in the rains of winter, and see the stems of wheat that fed people generations

Out of Reach

ago once more emerging into the light. And some of the seeds of wild plants we found in the clay bats grew when given the chance.

The little community in the fen was dead by the time we arrived. Traces lingered: along the high banks of the rivers at intervals slades went down to the floor of the fen, and up them, once, cargoes for the barges had been hauled from the farms. (In the mind's eye, as I walk those banks on a wild, bright March day, I can see the little sails the bargees used to help the boats along, and Captain the clever horse jumping the fences.) A few houses remained, mostly in ruins, gradually crumbling away into the tide of nettles that washes over land where humans have lived; as for those that were gone, even the field names that marked them, the drove names, are forgotten. Who now knows where Harrison's Rand took you?

Down on the riverbank was Pout Hall, two rooms, wooden, with a brick floor set in the black earth, and a brick chimney stack. It was probably built some time in the 1840s. Four sycamores protected it from the west, and it snuggled its back against the embankment of the river, ten feet above the fields at that spot.

I knew the last of the children who had been brought up in that house. I heard him speak of cutting the peats; I heard him speak of the great gangs of lighters, towed by a single horse or by a steam tug, that passed on their way up to Cambridge or, laden with sugar beet, to Ely. I saw the punt, hidden in the reeds like other punts before it, that allowed a quiet slipping over into the Nature Reserve on the other bank. But he and his family had long deserted Pout Hall for a council house some miles away, and had simply left - they took virtually nothing with them. So the house was open to any who passed, the only shelter along that long, bleak way between the villages. There was still a pianola, leaning over as the floor heaved, until in the end it toppled over with an unheard crash and jangle of strings. There were chairs, a bed. The boarding of the ceiling, good tongue-and-groove, would have been worth salvaging, but there was no road to the house. A few apple trees outside marked where the garden had been.

Do houses have memories? An old house like ours - once two houses - has seen much. During the 20s in one half of it - two rooms up, two down - a family brought up seven children: nothing unusual for the period in that, or in the wage of 25 shillings a week the man was earning. But how did those nine people build up the invisible walls that demarcated their own specialness when living so close to each other? What strains did the mother have to cope with, and how did she and he look back on the years when their children were growing? Unknowable, of course; but perhaps the house knows.

Verbal memory takes us back to second-remove contact with those folk. The house takes us further. That family, and the generations before them, chucked a lot of their rubbish over the hedge into the old dock running down beside the garden from the lane to the river. (Without the untidiness of countryfolk, archaeologists would be stuck for a job.) For years, horses coming off the fen used to be washed down there. Gradually, the water receded. The nettles and then the trees grew, and the dock, where once upon a time barges loaded stone for the building of Ely Cathedral, has become part of the garden, a place for wood-stacks, and beehives, an occasional hen-run. I have dug a good deal of it over, though it is not yet archaeological, so to speak. Old enamel saucepans, rusting through, and cast-iron pots broken at the cistern; pottery, cheap willow-pattern mainly, in plenty; stoneware jars and grey straight-sided marmalade pots, fluted, with the groove round the rim for the string that secured the waxed paper covering; huge, square, long-necked bottles that once held 'Flag' sauce; little, wide-necked bottles

Out of Reach

that once held the crystals of Wadsworth's Cambridge Lemonade. Beneath the roots of an elder tree, no crock of gold but a broken bit of blue-glazed German pottery of two centuries ago, with the story of 'Die schöne Susanna' and the naughty elders on it, rather explicitly. There are occasional blue bottles that once, by convention, held poison.

One early find was a reaping sickle, beautiful steel, that only needed sharpening, and a new handle to fit in the hand that would never use it seriously. Another was a pair of hand sheep-shears: one point was rusted through, but they sharpened up and their spring is still youthful enough to give a glimpse of how at the start of shearing a man's wrist would soon throb with swollen pain. (They hang on the wall of the workshop, their point tied with the traditional wisp of wool, in honour of those who once used them. I have not tried, as was traditional, to cut hair with them.) And then there are bones: half the skull of a cow, sawn through; several pig's jaws; the massive shank-bones of the ox - I can remember my parents boiling them for nourishing soup. (Another bit of the jigsaw completed. The pigs reared in the garden, killed at home, the mad activity with the neighbours to butcher the carcass, clean the chitterlings and offal, boil the head down for brawn, joint the meat and salt it down in the five-gallon porkpot I inherited and used for brewing beer.) Still digging, deeper, pottery that goes back to mediaeval times. I was shown a few years back the shards of one great pot that someone had dug up complete while digging foundations nearby: his son had used what looked to me like an ancient cinerary urn for target practice with his air rifle. (Like the coins Ben dug up, and gave to his children to play shop with.) And there is, too, a layer of ash that seems to underlie in the site. Is that a trace of the fire that burnt most of the village one night of gale in the 1850s? And what happened to the people, uninsured, homeless in October?

The remains do not tell that story. But curious things about the house suggest that the place remembers. Soon after we began modifications, we ripped out the second cupboard staircase, refloored upstairs, and soaked all the woodwork in

Out of Reach

preservative. With paint on top, the place smelt for weeks. Yet even now, years afterwards, one can occasionally go upstairs in the quiet of the evening and feel, almost, as if one is disturbing someone. The smell of Jeyes' Fluid, which we have never used, is at one spot sometimes overpowering. Steps are sometime heard on the gravel outside - yet there has been no gravel there for twenty years. And more tangibly, one sees everywhere in the garden, in the turned earth, in the rubbish, the relics of lives long gone.

We are adding our signatures to the palimpsest, of course. Years ago I took out a window and built in a new one. I finished off round it with Polyfilla, decorated, and thought no more about it. Then, last year, that room had to be redecorated, and under the wallpaper, scratched into the Polyfilla when it had been wet was the remark, 'Dad is a very messy painter.' It is true enough; but what, I wonder, will some future owner speculate about that? It is disconcerting enough to see ourselves as we were seen by our children before the age of discretion.

Over the years, I have seen the land heave and slowly shrug Pout Hall off its back. The roof blew off; the ceilings fell, someone made a fire to warm themselves with the bits of the pianola (but there were still playing cards and Wills' cigarette cards in the gaping drawer in the room where the bed had been). The stack leaned, the mortar between the bricks washed away, a kestrel nested in the sycamores. The waves of nettles broke round the island that man had made. Now only the sycamores and the apples remain, and in the spring, where the house stood, the only memorial is a carpet of snowdrops under the trees, growing in the regular clumps that indicate that they have been there a very long time. The house is gone, like all the other houses whose lamps once pinpricked the darkness of the fen in winter; but the land is slow to forget wholly those who lived on it.

Out of Reach

The old ones would spin like teetotums in their graves if they saw what was happening in the fen now. They knew how hard it was to dry that land, and keep it dry. They knew how to wring the last little bit of produce out of it. Thus the contradictory feeling many of them, like Harold, had for the Nature Reserve: a relic of a landscape, and a way of life, that marched with memories of their youth, but an affront to their sense of what was proper. No appeals to conservation values, or the value of wilderness, would have cut any ice with them.

But now: vast acres of the fen, which grew wheat, potatoes, barley, sugar beet, and back to wheat, are down to, of all things, lawn turf: a monoculture that feeds nobody, that offers no cover to any creeping thing, that is weedkilled so often that not even mushrooms will grow on it. And bit by bit that black soil is mined, and carted away with the rolled turf to grace a golf-course green or whatever. Sheep have returned to land that has not seen them for three generations of men: to make cheese. The park in the next village, where fat beeves grazed richly only half a dozen years ago, is home to a herd of red deer. Or the field by the river, where that morning long ago I watched Seth shoot that pheasant: that is now excavated to form a pool, with an island for breeding birds. Reeds and osiers and other wet-loving plants are planted deliberately where twenty years ago they were ruthlessly grubbed up. I am delighted to see the snipe there, to hear the geese flighting - but in my mind I keep hearing a voice that sounds like Seth's saying, 'A terrible lot of people went hungry.' I hear the lark ascending from a field in setaside, and rejoice, and at dusk may catch a glimpse of her grace the barn owl. But I see the thistles are growing straight and tall, and I think this cannot be keeping faith with those long dead who sweated to clean this land.

You can still stand at the edge of the high land and look out

Out of Reach

across the level fen, and there nothing interrupts your gaze - hardly a tree, hardly a hedge - until your eye travels the low swelling of the Isle of Ely six miles away. Between you and that horizon, on that land plotted and pieced into the most productive fields in England, it would seem no mystery could dwell. I am not so sure. You can feel as remote from human kind down that fen, glimpsing even the classic Panic terror, as on any Scottish hill or Arctic icecap - and I have been on both. And the land has its secrets, and its secret memories, traces of which it sometimes gives up.

Behind Toby's shop, on the wall of his courtyard, hung a piece of deer antler. It now sits on top of the bookcase in my study. It is about half of the whole, I imagine. The beast that cast it was bigger than any red deer stag I have ever seen, for the first branch of the antler is a good two inches in diameter. Toby found it, as a young man, when he was ploughing in the fen. The break may have happened when the Suffolk's great hoofs trod on it. The proud beast that wore it for a season had been gone for many hundreds of years, and the world it roamed in remained only in the fallen trunks of the forest that lay beneath the blanket of peat.

I coveted that antler: I coveted it for the lost, unknowable world it recalled, the sheer heavy age of the thing in one's hands. And Toby knew it. He was the most generous of men. But he only gave it me on the last day he lived in the village, as he gave up the shop. At the same time, he gave me the wooden till that his mother had used. He handed it over, I think, to mark the closing of a chapter of his life as another was opening. He gave it to us, he said, because he could not put 'that old thing' in a new modern house, whither he was going. I think there was more to it than that.

When it got to be known that we were interested in old things, people began to bring all sorts to us. And so we began to realise we had been wrong about a lot of things and a lot of people. Many men who worked on the land may have had scant idea of history, but they recognised the labour of men's hands when they saw it, and venerated it. There was Bob, with his collection of bronze axes, each of which, in years

Out of Reach

long gone, he had ploughed out of the black soil. He had mounted them with cord on a board, framed them, and then hung them on the wall above the tiled fireplace in his bungalow. (And the fire burned bog-oak.) There was John, with an eye that could spot a worked flint at twenty yards after rain on the tilled surface. And Frank, who brought to our door, and left, one of our greatest treasures: a Bronze-Age stone axe which he had just ploughed out of the fen. It has been identified as one of those made in Great Langdale.

One kept on being nudged by the past, as if it was just out of vision, at the tail of the eye, gone as soon as you turned to look at it. There are stories - some impossible - of the finding of bog-bodies in Burwell Fen - one of a man standing upright in a canoe. But people must have got lost in the fen, and floundered into the quagmires, and drowned, and somewhere those bodies would lie uncorrupted in the blanket of the peat for ages to come. But it is the remnants of their tools, the hints of their quarry, that even today still surface to remind us that we are tenants for a spell, not owners of this land.

Sometimes something happens to bring home forcefully life of a world man rarely sees, or has forgotten. Jenny and I were walking across the fen one spring day, when suddenly, upwind of us, was a roebuck peacefully grazing on the sugar beet. Later we found his slot leading back into the fastnesses of the Nature Reserve - a wilderness those bog people might have found familiar. Nobody knew they were there. Another time, miles down the fen, along the riverbank, I found the unmistakable slot of a red deer: the beast had clearly swum the river, come down the bank - the wet around showed where he slipped at one point - and galloped off across the black earth. The nakedness of the land would not hide a mouse, one thinks. But that secret life goes on. Few are about to see it, but it waits in the wings until we have finished.

Driving Justin to school one morning, I stop in Swaffham to

Out of Reach

pick up other boys bound for Cambridge. On Elizabeth's kitchen table, next to the boys' satchels, is a box with some brown bones sticking out of it. The boys' oblivious chatter carries on, and silently Elizabeth lifts out first one, then another: a femur, and a damaged skull. 'John Clarke found them yesterday ploughing that bit next to the Ditch. Probably Iron Age.' But we are getting late, and must be off: there is Cambridge traffic to fight through. No time to talk more: and I never did find out what happened to those bones. Their owner probably once thought he owned this land.

Chapter Ten

Coming from a county where farming means sheep and cows and only occasional arable, many things were unfamiliar to us. We had never been in a countryside where the summer turned most of the land to gold, and then the combines crawled across the level fields grazing the corn to stubble. We had never seen before the angry towers of smoke rising into the hot sky from the lines of straw which the machines excreted. For there was no use for the straw, least of all after it was chewed up by the combine. (Yet at the turn of the century a farmer could grow wheat and make his money by selling the long, straight straw for thatching: anything he got for the grain was a bonus.) At night, the long lines of burning straw across the fields lit up the dark, and every so often the bigger heaps where the combines turned sent flames shooting higher into the sky. There is no doubt it was beautiful - and enjoyable, both to watch and to light. (I was once in the nick of time to stop Justin and an importunate friend setting light to the stubble of our allotment, just combined: there was standing corn for miles, and a merry wind. That sort of memory still makes me curl my toes. . . .) We all are closet pyromaniacs, and at harvest time those fires perhaps spoke, like Guy Fawkes' Night, to the sleeping primitive in all of us who would light his Samhain fires to honour the dead; or just for fun. The threshold of winter, the cleansing. 'Yew gits rid of a terrible lot of seeds that way,' said Seth as we lit the three rows of straw the combine had left on his little patch of land, and indeed, you do: Vergil says so as well. But he was really, I am sure, making an excuse for enjoying it.

But sometimes, in a dry year, the fires took hold on the peat itself, and even found a piece of oak lurking beneath the surface, dry enough to take fire and smoulder. If it was a

Out of Reach

really big trunk, the fire could eat its way in for yards under the soil, almost unseen: no flame, no smoke, only a pervading bitter-sweetness that could be smelt on the wind two fields away - and steam when the rains of October started. But once 'pitted in', a big fen fire would burn for weeks, months even, and some would not die until they had burned themselves right out, or a big snowfall came to smother them. To try to put them out, to dig them out, might only make things worse by increasing the supply of air to the fire. And so the fire down below burned, and those who knew trod warily round it. For not seldom the surface of the land would look as if nothing was amiss, yet it was a thin crust over the furnace. Men, and animals, had been known to fall in: when the sudden rush of air let the pent-up gas explode with a blue flash and a 'whoosh': and then the scream.

It does not happen now: or not much. The last fen fire I saw was caused by a group of youths, joyriding in a stolen car, and then abandoning and firing it down the fen.

My parents are down from Lancashire on their first visit, just after harvest. The meal is over, and the gathered dusk invites a quiet smoke outside. The northern horizon is ringed with stubble fires. And my mother suddenly shudders: 'It's just like the Blitz' - for to her this brings back with unexpected intensity the year I was born, the nights of bombing and terror and dogged determination in Manchester. And my father reminds her of her aged mother, born in another age, standing in the garden in Fallowfield refusing to enter the Anderson shelter just yet, looking north at Manchester burning, and saying, 'O Tom, isn't it beautiful!'

Out of Reach

And harvest comes, and goes, and the fieldfares arrive as the days noticeably shorten. Winter in East Anglia can searingly cold. You get used to it, sort of. Sometimes the wind goes into the north-east or east, and blows for days or end with grey overcast - a wind straight from the Urals, as Kate used to say, only she called them 'the Urinals'; a wind that shrivels the marrow of your bones. There are some winters, though, that stand out. That morning, for instance, when Justin and I went out at dawn in the snow to shoot, and the whole place was frozen into stillness. My left hand stuck to my gun barrels. Far overhead, where the sun was lighting them up, a couple of swans flew in unison, but too high for us to hear the music of their wings. A crack like a shot as the sap froze in a tree.

Or another winter, a late afternoon, as sharp in the mind now as if I could feel the frost on my fingers. The river is frozen, and everyone - the entire village - is playing. Tubby Derek, usually surly, gliding by on his father's skates, his flat cap still at the usual truculent angle, but smiling and affable. Old Harold Sennett, as round as he is tall, a thing of infinite grace, swooping by bent double, arms behind his back in the old fen fashion, on his long fen runners, cap at jaunty angle over his deep-set black eyes. A swallow among sparrows: for the children are sliding about and getting in everyone's way, including Jenny's, who is using a chair as a Zimmer frame. The younger end, boys and girls together, are showing off to each other with a to-be-noticed hilarity, like the figures in the corners of an Avercamp winter scene. In among all this, romping with excitement, unchecked, cavort three dogs, engaged in unspeakable but all too visible pursuits. The sun goes down over the black fen the colour of the rose hips that still linger on the dog roses in the hedge, and the first star appears. With the sun, the temperature sinks noticeably, but the sound of young laughter echoes for long yet across the frozen fields.

We get little snow here - the East Anglian Heights catch it when it comes from the east or north, and when it comes from the west it is more or less all used up by the long trek

Out of Reach

across England. But the frost can be sharp indeed. Life can present hard choices when the bucket in an outside privy freezes into a solid lump: I have known it happen. Or, working a boat down the river where it is tidal, the diesel freezing, and the boat suddenly helpless in the stream - it happened one January to Justin. Such cold is rare, to be sure; but many East Anglian winters have at least a few days of serious cold. One morning in one of the hard Januaries of the early '80s, Don came in for a warm after being out lifting sugar beet with Justin - a thankless, mucky job at the best of times. Conversation is not his strong point. The usual silence, with me, whose job is words, worrying that I ought to be saying something, but I cannot think what, for every lob to him drops flat. But then: 'Bit cold last night'. (It had been, indeed: ten degrees Fahrenheit.) Pause.

'Dew yew knaow, when I woke up this morning me teeth were froazen in me glaass.'

I dared not look at Justin, for it was clearly not meant to be funny. It was a practical consideration, indeed, for the house that Don shared with his father had no insulation, and little heating. But how do you reply to such a gambit? And we did not dare ask how he extracted them from the block of ice, even though he gleamingly had done. Nor did we ever learn.

In that bare countryside, naked of crops after harvest, at nightfall the wildlife makes for the little pockets of cover that remain - the ditch-banks, the few scraggy, grown-out hedges, a patch of scrub on a corner of land that nobody's machines can get at. The partridges settle quietly in their outward-facing coveys in the open ground, for they are well camouflaged, and their individual safety lies in being in a group whose members can take off instantly in all directions. Pheasants walk across the open ground circumspectly enough, only to tell everyone where they are at the last

Out of Reach

minute when with a clatter and their territorial squawk ('KekKeK') they rocket into the bush or tree, where they croon quietly to themselves before settling down to roost Many times have I stood quietly, well camouflaged, under a tree at nightfall with a pheasant a few feet above me making that extraordinary, and beautiful, noise.

There were ways of taking 'buds' without a gun. 'Guns? Naow, too much noise', said Bill Gathercole to me one time. It was late one winter afternoon, and we were looking across the fen to the line of blackthorn bushes that had grown up along where the railway line used to be. In the still air we could hear the pheasants clattering into the bushes one after another: later I used to rabbit along those bushes, forcing my way through the intervening brambles, and there might be fifty birds in as many yards on a still night.

'So how?' I asked.

'Terbakker tin and a chewb,' was the mysterious reply.

He rolled a cigarette from his tin of Old Holborn, and I stood silent, half-expecting him to perform this miracle before my very eyes. Deliberately, he licked the paper, shut the tin, put it back in his pocket.

'Syrup tin'll dew,' he said.

Pause. Then comes the explanation. Take a long - six feet at least - piece of bamboo, or even several joints of a set of bamboo drain rods. Bore out the joints, so the whole is hollow. Take a piece of sacking or rag, and some of the sulphur you could (then) get from most chemists. Soak the cloth in the sulphur, and put it in the tin. You will have punched ventilation holes in the bottom and sides of this, and a hole in the top into which the bottom of your tube will fit nicely. You light the rags, so that they smoulder quietly. Then, as silently as you can, make your way to the thicket in the dark and choose your sleeping bird. Fix the tube into the top hole, and blow through the ventilation holes. The fire will grow, and as it does, gently move the top of the tube to under the bird, under its head, if possible. It will have sweet dreams, and never know its end. It tumbles limp off the branch: a quick twist, and into the sack with it.

I did not believe this: I thought I was having my leg pulled again - even more when Bill volunteered the reassuring information that 'that old smoke dun't taste the buds'. But I have since heard this story supported several times, and once upon a time I would have been inclined to try it. Even then, though, I suspect my younger body might not have had the stealth to move silently in brittle undergrowth, and leave the company of pheasants asleep as I blew up their doom.

I never knew how much Ben, and Seth, and Bill, and the others pulled my leg. Certainly, I could never get some of the tricks they put me up to to work. Perhaps I was just clumsy - or had not the bred-in patience of the born-to-it hunter. Seth swore he could take a hare without snare or dog or gun and, to be sure, I have seen him come up the fen with none of those things, but with the sack over his handlebars heavy with the smooth curve of the back of something about the size of a hare.

'First catch your hare. . .' Hares, disturbed, will take off like a rocket. But then, after a spurt of a hundred yards or more, if they are not chased, they will very often stop, and look back, to see what it was that frightened them. And they do like to keep on their own bit of territory, unless it is springtime, when they congregate for the karate matches that are part of their mating ritual. It is this habit that Seth said he could use.

'All yew need is a stick, mate. Any old stick. Jest yew stick that in the grund, and hang y' coat on it. That old hare, he'll keep on lookin' at that coat, 'cos that's what frit 'im. Now, dew yew walk away from that coat, and round in a big circle, and yew'll git behind that old boy, and yew can get up real

Out of Reach

close, and grab 'im before he know where yew are.'

Perhaps. I never made it work, but the hares did sit and watch for a time. Puzzled, perhaps.

These tricks were wholly necessary to the generation that drew its pension as ours started to earn. 'Eight hundred men out of work in Soham': that memory died hard. And before that, their fathers remembered the lockouts, when the farmers in the 1870s banded together against their men forming a union. Newmarket was where, in 1874, the farmers formed their association to break the union, and the terrible rift between master and man grew bitter and beyond forgetting. There were men and women in the villages round about who knew Joseph Arch's ironic grace, dating from those troubled times of rick-burning and hunger, of wages forced down, and virtually no chance of any family not at some point drawing on parish relief.

> O Heavenly Father bless us,
> And keep us all alive;
> There are ten of us to dinner,
> And food for only five.

Wife and children had to get out and work, the women in season hoeing corn or turnips or potatoes, or gleaning; the very young children scaring birds. A few pennies a week made all the difference. Perhaps, with no work, and infinite time, I might have got the knack of taking a hare in Seth's way. I would have had to.

A lot of the old folk, who had to poach to keep a family, used to poach at night. Some, quite recently, though not, 1 think, in my time, used the old method of the net. The long net, about six feet by fifty yards, could be wound round the body for concealment as you went out for an evening stroll with your mate. Then, having found a likely field, the two of you

Out of Reach

would quietly unfurl the net, stretch it out, and walk quietly down the field dragging it along. The partridge and the hare would sit tight until too late, and another family was fed. Or again, several men told me they could call pheasants down out of a tree, and it is true that I have heard men make peculiar noises that the birds have answered, though I have never seen the trick done, and try as I can I cannot make the same noises myself. Seth used to say the fox could mesmerise the birds to come down, and I have heard the story elsewhere: I don't know, but it does seem to occur in mediaeval carvings and some beast stories. But who was watching the procedure?

Standing quietly under the eaves of a spinney, or in a ditch, at the thickening of the light towards dusk, you see at lot of wildlife. A lot of birds were quietly, and not so quietly, taken. A gun is a noisy thing, and catapults, and nooses, were favoured for roosting birds. Another trick, confirmed by my old cousin who farmed up on the slopes of the Pennines, was to soak raisins in beer, and spread them in the lee of a hedge at night. In the morning, the pheasants were so drunk they could simply be picked up. Seth's winter trick, when there was snow on the ground, was to find a drift near a bit of cover and with a bottle make some holes in it about eight inches deep. A raisin or two at the bottom of the hole, along comes the pheasant, stretches to reach his favourite food, and bingo! he's upside down, and incapable, with his neck in the hole and his feet in the air. (That one works.)

We were poor. For the first years we lived in the village the only butcher's meat we could afford was breast of lamb at half-a-crown a go. So growing our own food, and getting as much as we could off the fen, was a priority, and the legality we did not worry too much about - nor had anyone else in that house before us. Growing vegetables became one of the major chores, and, of course, we knew little about how to set to work. We knew one planted in spring, or thereabouts, and that was about it.

Out of Reach

The first Eastertide we spent in the house was grey and bitter. I can recall several Easters when snow flurries darkened the north-eastern sky. For here the spring can come slowly indeed when the continental high sits glowering over Germany, and the easterly - 'no good to man nor beast' - brings its blanket of stubborn grey cloud for a whole moon at a time. But Easter time was the traditional season for cottagers and labourers to get much of their planting done, and when later we came to have an allotment we too tried to set our land in due time and order. So a cold Easter might still find us working the land to a fine tilth if it was dry enough, planting onion sets and seed, and putting in the spuds.

We often had neighbours say to us, 'Plant y'spuds on Good Friday. Dun't, them'll never make much.' We assumed that behind this lay some superstition about lucky and unlucky days - *dies nefas*. But in fact it was originally no such thing: the custom, still adhered to, of planting on Good Friday stemmed from the fact that, in the years up to the last war, on that day only farmers might be persuaded to lend a horse for the business of trenching and ridging - provided the animal was back in the stable by 'Church time' - usually 11am. Planting enough spuds to keep a large family through the year must have meant a terribly early start. Anyway, we planted about Easter, and sometimes we were lucky and they grew and luxuriated, and cropped gigantically, and other years they were nasty thrawn little things, with yellowing leaves and slug-galleried tubers. As always, I was often 'in too much of bloody 'urry', and took a chance on the weather, trusting it would stay, or get, warm. We have too often gone down to the land on a spring evening to see the fleshy tops just pushing through the earth, and patted ourselves on the back for having the earliest spuds in the village - and then, next morning, found them all black and withered with the night's frost.

It was Ben who took me in hand, after about the third year of complaints.

'Too much of an 'urry, mate. Yew wait till the land's right, yew'll get those old plants going jest as soon.'

Out of Reach

But how did one know when it was warm enough?

'Easy. Jest yew goo on y'land, and if that dun't stick to y'boots it's dry enough, and if yew takes y'trousers down, and sits on the ridges, and that dun't feel cold, that's warm enough.'

No leg-pull, I was assured; and, indeed, the advice is recorded from many places besides this parish. The experience, if one does wait, is not wholly unpleasant.

But growing food on a scale to feed a family, even a small one like ours, is hard work, and the reminder of it ahead, after a day's work, is always there in the hard patches on the hands, perpetually stained with soil, that scrape across the paper as one writes. And though we needed to do it, we were not utterly dependent on it as the former dwellers in our house, on our land, had been. For them, the allotment and its working were inexorable, even if, as happened, the farmer might lend a horse. And some did not. And so a peasant community like ours had tools and things that have now, I think, almost vanished elsewhere. When we first knew him, George each spring used to root in the back of his green corrugated-iron shed and pull out a breast-plough - very like the caschcrom of the Hebrides. Leaning on this, driving its blade before him through the earth of his yard - East Anglia, like the USA, calls gardens yards - he would turn it over with shallow furrows. Later, out would come the wheeled 'Planet' patent hoe - I have one myself - which comes into its own with long straight rows of corn or seedling beet, where the two blades can run just under the surface on each side of the plants. Other villagers reminisced about the donkey plough that so-and-so used to use, of one intelligent sow that was taught to pull a plough, and so on; behind it all was the need to do the work, and the harsh truth of its hardness.

But its joys too. For the first fruits are indeed a joy, a sacrament - wisely did our fathers offer the first fruits as a grateful sacrifice. I remember the first time I felt that joy. Down on Seth's land. The eruption, prompted by the fork, of huge golden potatoes from the black soil. Seth replaced the tools in the engineless, tyreless, Riley car that stood, with only one

Out of Reach

seat left, under the greengage tree in the corner of his land. (The only car Seth ever owned, doing him good service as a toolshed and shelter from a sudden shower. And as a hide from which to shoot occasionally.) ''Ere: tek these.' They were a bond between us. And one day, some years later, as I dug the first new potatoes from my land while my father watched, I hit a nerve of painful pleasure, that took him back to his own unnarrated youth, digging spuds with his father: 'Billy Moseley will never be dead as long as you are growing spuds'. Was it pride? Grieving, even after all those years? (I do not think they were ever close.) I do not know. But we were silent on the walk back, with the happy burden shared between us.

Growing vegetables eventually became a delight, year after year, till I came to take pride in growing what were acknowledged - grudgingly, for was I not a foreigner? - to be good vegetables. One proud moment: I was bringing a load of onions home from the allotment, and though I say it myself, they were, as usual, champion onions. But that year those Ailsa Craigs were spectacular: firm, bright gold, many of their buxom globes weighed in at nearly a pound. George looked at them from over his gate, and did not hide his admiration.

'Where d'yew git the seed?'

I told him. And his comment warms my heart as it underlines the different worlds we inhabit. 'Dew yew goo and show him those: best onions I've seen for many a day. He might give yew half a crown, like as not.'

George's world was one where a seedsman would make a reputation on what people made of his wares: and pay for specimens to exhibit. But what would I do with half-a-crown?

We took on an acre of allotment and grew a small cash crop. We even made bread - once - from our own wheat, and with some pride spread a table for our friends where every

Out of Reach

single thing in the meal except the salt had been produced on our land by our labour, or gathered by our hands in the neighbourhood. A fire burned on our hearth with wood we had cut ourselves. (But grinding wheat to flour in a coffee grinder is a slow business, and does not make very good flour. The bread was nutritious but solid.)

These were good feelings. We might have felt differently about it if we had had absolutely no option.

Meat in the early days was more of a problem than greens and fruit, and so I too, like folk in that house before me, me to take my stand at evenfall in the lee of the hedge, or in the spinney, alert and silent, as much a predator as a cat on the hunt. Many times, particularly in the early days, I came home with nothing; but increasingly often a rabbit betrayed by his white scut bobbing in the gloaming, or a cock pheasant that had been on his way to bed (I tried not to take hens), warmed my side as I trudged home after full dark. I remember the very first rabbit, laying it proudly down in the kitchen, and little Antonia laughing with delight as she stroked its soft fur. (Another rug that did not get finished.)

Justin, of course, was all too keen to join in, and when quite small used to tag along. (So did the cat of that time, which had been abandoned by its mother and had been brought up by the labrador.) Many a son in the village had similarly accompanied his father over the years, and Justin became, through early training, better able to move silently and unseen through the countryside than I shall ever be. Of course he was too young for a gun. But he was not too young for a catapult. And I remember us coming home one evening, to a son beaming from ear to ear, who took us into the shed where lay something covered with a cloth. With a flourish, and no word, he whisked the cloth away: there was his first pheasant, got with his catapult at close range while roosting. Who would begrudge him that joy?

Out of Reach

Plenty would, of course, in the name of all sorts of morality. So we were always careful, as Seth and Ben had taught us, to be discreet, not to be seen more than could be helped - just as everyone else played the same game. Occasionally, of course, this led to comedy.

A thicket at nightfall, with me silently at the edge, face masked so as not to show up, waiting for whatever came, and suddenly I hear in the thicket a twig snap and a soft oath. Someone else at the same game. So I cough. Each of us knows the other is there, and has a pretty good idea who the other is: but the convention is to ignore each other, and we do. But neither of us shoots, and the birds have a quiet evening, after all.

The time came quite early, of course, when I reasoned Jenny into agreeing that if we were going to be successful with this business of finding game I needed a dog. A dog was supposed to help catch food: to flush birds out of cover, to start hares or rabbits, to retrieve what had been shot. Gunnar came of a noble lineage - Jenny's parents' generosity allowed for that. But he did not impress Seth. 'Might as well have a grut donkey in the house as that useless bugger', was one of the kinder, first, comments on this leggy, enthusiastic, tireless animal. And Gunnar loved Seth, loved him to the point where he would lie on his coat, carefully folded and laid aside as he worked, to guard it. He would pick it up in his mouth and bring it to him when he least wanted it. Seth was not pleased: 'Git off me good coat, yew bugger.' (That coat, folded, showed the wartime 'CC' utility mark on its lining - all of twenty years old. Cheap clothing, and the mindset it induced, had not yet arrived.) For every curse Seth's gruffness gave the dog, the tail wagged the more, and the brown eyes adored.

But Gunnar had his drawbacks, and his own opinions, as a hunting dog. When he was still young, I sent him to get a

Out of Reach

duck that I had shot. It had fallen in the middle of a pond. He tried: how he tried, but he could not manage to grasp that bird. He pushed it with his nose, and the duck bobbed away. It seemed to sink lower and lower in the water as time and again he pushed it round that pond - never towards the bank until the very last minute, and then it was the one furthest away from me. Then there was one bitter night of sleet and gusty westerly, when far down the fen I shot a duck. It fell on the other side of the Engine Drain: ten feet down to the water, three or four yards to swim, and a steep scramble up the far bank. Gunnar saw it fall. He went to the edge of the Engine Drain, and stood, his ears blown back in the wind. Then sat down. No threats, cajoling, no throwing of clods over the water, would change his opinion: he had had enough, and if I wanted that duck, I could go and get it. In the end, glad that there was nobody to see me, watched by the dog, I put the gun down and went into the freezing water, and up the other bank. And I can see now why Seth was so scathing about me and my dog. Who would go stalking - which is what I was doing, rather than using him as he was bred to be - with a bright yellow Lab? A dog whose pleasure in the proceedings was so obvious that, when told to sit still and be quiet, his excited pants smoked a little cloud, which could be seen for half a mile, into the frosty air.

Sometimes a few of the men would get together for a spot of legitimate shooting - walking a patch of sugar beet, for example, or following the combines round the ever-shrinking island of corn. Sometimes such shooting parties ended in farce that nearly was something else. Ben told me how he and three others had been down the fen one Sunday morning after something for the pot - shooting on Sunday was still illegal then - when a private plane from the nearby airfield started buzzing them, and driving any game miles away. It was quite probably someone who thought it was a huge joke, or someone who disapproved of shooting.

'Well, bugger me,' says Ben, 'we di'n't like that one little bit, mate - bit too like those bloody Gerries in the war.' (They had all been in the forces.) 'So we just ups with the old guns and lets him have it. 'Course, we couldn't do much damage at that range, but he soon takes off and leaves us alone.'

I imagine he did. I heard the sequel from Ben's wife later. The men carried on, until one of them heard a police siren; and then another siren, and another. They realised that it must be to do with them, and that the pilot had gone back in alarm to report them. So they split up, and slipped into the ditches, which criss-cross the fen and are deeper than a man is tall in most places. Each man made his own way home circuitously, through the maze of muddy, reedy seams that knit the drained land together, and found a policeman waiting for him at home. But as he was alone, and the pilot had seen four men together, there was nothing the police could do. 'And', said Phil, 'you could see they di'n't mind.' The policeman then still had an easy relationship with the community he served. He could act, very often, on his own initiative, dispensing summary justice to the young whom he had watched grow up, without benefit of magistrates and probation officers and the scarring, confrontational, rigmarole of official procedures. Many were just men, and could count on the support of the community and the support of those they chastised as they grew up. A few nice stories were told of the bobby from the next village: when he retired, the policing was done by anonymous men, masked in cars, who did not know the place and who were universally regarded as outsiders, not to be cooperated with. No stories about them.

Bill Bailey's exploits, as he reported them, challenged even Seth's. His cottage down the fen was a clutter, inside and out, of eel-grigs, partridge nets, turf beckets, punt-guns, old twelve- and ten-bores. The Nature Reserve was for him a

Out of Reach

happy hunting ground, and many a time he was glimpsed among the reeds in his thigh boots, with his gun. He was indeed a splendid shot. One time the bobby thought he had got him. He met him walking through the village with a bulge in his coat and a pheasant tail poking through an unnoticed hole in the lining.

'Where yew goin' with that old bird, Bill? Yew've got no licence for 'em.'

'Jest coming to see yew, constable - long time since I give yew a dinner, and I jest happened to find this old bird someone had shot.' (The policeman preferred the dinner.)

But one night the bobby heard a couple of shots, and spotted him at the end of the Reserve. He gave chase: all part of the fun, and to catch wily old Bill would be a triumph. Well, Bill ran home in his tall boots, threw his gun in the corner of the kitchen, and breathlessly said to his wife, 'I bin in all evening'. He dashed upstairs and got into bed just as he was. Mrs Bill told the story with relish.

'In come that copper, says "Where's Bill?" and I say "He bin in all evening, he's sick, real bad, and in bed upstairs, yew can go an see him." So up he go, and I hear him say, "Funny, Bill, could have swore that wor yew down the fen jest now." "O no," says my Bill, "I bin sick real bad: bin here all day." So then that old copper reaches over and pulls down the bedclothes, and there's Bill in bed with his waders on. And copper says to him "Dew yew allus goo to bed like this, Bill?" and Bill says, "No, only in the winter time."' Bill got off that time too.

Like Seth, Bill was a natural storyteller, with an eye for the plausibly incredible. 'There I wor, lovely afternoon, cleaning me gun by the fire, and I looks out the winder, and sees a flight of duck and I can see them'll pass over the chimney directly. So I puts me gun together and shoves a couple up the spout, and fires both up the chimney. Dew yew knaow, bor, four duck fall, and three fall on a patch of mushrooms and the other falls on the neck of a hare and kills it.' That story was still going the rounds long after Bill died.

Out of Reach

Chapter Eleven

Bury Market, on Wednesdays, was much preferred to Cambridge. A special bus collected people from the villages and, with lots of other special buses from all over Suffolk, decanted them into the town by late morning. By lunchtime on those days, the town was full to bursting: Bury's population was suddenly, temporarily, not 'small market' (with pretensions to elegance), but wholly 'country', the acme of smartness being the clean cap and the gumboots kept and polished specially for market days. The pubs stayed open all day, and passing the open doors and windows the noise and smell of tightly packed men drinking beer overwhelmed all other senses. Their wives, meanwhile, foraged through the stalls that filled the marketplace: cheap lingerie in frilly black and red being bought by large ladies with faces round and rosy like a Cox's apple, vegetables, fish, shoes, household goods, cheese, gifts ('could not do it this price usually'), ironmongery, rugs, wickerware, car accessories. Cattle trucks - within memory the animals would have walked there - filled the streets leading to the market, with frightened eyes peering through the ventilation slits, and the ammoniacal whiff of cattle stale throbbing at traffic lights. If the wind was in the north and it was winter, when the sugar beet was being lifted, the sickly toffee smell of the refinery got into everything.

Sooner or later most people gravitated up the hill to the cattle market and the auctions. You could buy an oil painting, or a set of antique china, or a broken bicycle, or a mahogany corner cupboard, or a chainsaw minus its chain, or a lawnmower, or children's toys. You could rootle among the rows of boxes laid out for inspection, and find a pack of six-inch bolts, or a set of spanners, or a box of books, and sometimes in among the slag of Mills and Boons you found a glint of

Out of Reach

gold: an old Everyman, or a Temple Classic, or even better.

Or, as I used to with the children, you could walk through the loud lines of pig pens (the smell and the noise unlike any others), their occupants, like pigs everywhere, very tight to their own concerns, then through the softer pens of sheep (worried hoofs clicking on the concrete), into the sale shed. You sat in a miniature amphitheatre holding fifty at most; the seats rose in semicircular tiers. And one by one the bullocks would be goaded in, their weight announced, and made to circle the little orchestra, in front of the auctioneer's altar. The hot hay breath reached you in the front row, the eyes of the animal (ungarlanded) rolled so the whites showed in fear. No noise except its breathing and shambling, and the auctioneer picking up the bids of raised eyebrow or scratched nose. The assistant, a little brown man in a brown mac far too big for him and a brown flat cap too small, spat in the straw as each animal left; his stick a piece of ash cut from a hedge, smoothed and darkened with years of use. A nail was whipped to its end with a bit of tarred baler twine. He was there for years, and then suddenly, one Christmas, he was there no more. I wonder what he weighed and what he fetched...

The produce auction, especially at Christmas, was where you bought your poultry. Six hundred or so turkeys, a couple of hundred capons and cockerels, a few dozen geese - big money even when the prices were down, as they always were if you listened to the sellers. The crowd would start to gather a few minutes before the sale opened, beneath a big Dutch barn roof under which the winter wind could cast flurries of snow on the serried lines of naked corpses, their legs and wings so folded as the make the breasts appear plump to obscenity. 'Cut and come agin birds', as the auctioneer called them. Festive indeed; and the air was full of the scent of fish and chips, for there was a 'chippie' by the market which did incessant business on market days. The crush was tremendous: in the sales before Christmas, the press was so great that raising an arm to bid, as the inexperienced tried to, was virtually impossible. The nose received a fugue of smells, nice and

Out of Reach

nasty, of other human beings, while under all was the ground bass of dead poultry and the sweetish obbligato of poultry muck.

When bidding began, things suddenly became serious. Rapt attention, almost like in a poker game, faces as impassive: the auctioneer alert, his eyes hawking after the flicker of bids. Sometimes you could guess that a seller was attempting to force the price up, and risking buying his own birds back; sometimes you could see a little game being played, where a buyer was being teased into paying a higher price - 'taking him up' was the expression. You wasted, I suppose, a good deal of time, for auctions are slow things.

But cast your eye round; here a round man, with a wart on the cop right of his nose, like Chaucer's Miller; here is one with eyen glaring as an hare, like the Monk, especially when he looks across at the over-dressed, over-scented, over-painted Wife of Bath who appears every year and seems to know a lot of the men rather well. (Whom do *I* resemble?) You see all sorts at a poultry auction. Or the auctioneer's man, who holds up the birds for all to see as they are sold: big, beefy, dark, eyes like pebbles, a mouth like a gin trap concealing improbably perfect teeth, a horizontal fold of skin where nose meets forehead: he could have modelled in the crowd at a Bosch Crucifixion. The continuity with that ancient world is complete; and we prepare for the Nativity in a shed with a hole in the roof, straw round our feet, the east wind, and the canny cupidity of the peasant showing on every face.

It took us years to go to Bury Market, but once we did, we kept on going. You could buy almond-smelling russets, best of all Christmas apples; you could buy celery with the black earth of the fens still on its fluted ivory, or chestnuts, or cheeses to make your toes curl. It was Ben first persuaded us. Ben and Phil had a large plot of land quite near us, and he was not well off: in and out of work, he had to make his land feed himself and his wife and his four children. When he first lost his job, they decided hens were not enough: ducks would add variety to the diet and perhaps the eggs might bring in a bit of money. So off they went to Bury Market on

Out of Reach

Wednesday, and up to the produce auction. Round the ranks of dead birds are cages, four high, of live ones, forming a sort of outer wall to the open shed: guinea fowl, bantams (later we bought some of those ourselves), comfortable old hens that someone was hoping to pass off as point-of-lay birds (one trick to encourage bids was to put an egg, which might be hard-boiled, in the cage), pullets, pigeons, dirty ducks, and smirched geese with their imperturbable blue eyes haughtily surveying the squalor in which they unaccountably found themselves. Ben was after four ducks, and selected a pen of four to bid for. His bid, quite low, was accepted. 'How many?' said the auctioneer. 'Four', said Ben, mightily pleased. And at the end of the sale he went to pay for his four ducks . . . only to find that what he thought was a bid for one duck was a bid for one pen, and he was now the owner of four pens of ducks, totalling twenty birds in all.

Now how do you move twenty ducks when you came prepared for four? You cannot walk them home, as might have been done even sixty years ago; there was little traffic then. So you back your old car up to the pens, and you stuff each duck, with a fearful quacking and a spraying of excrement and a beating of wings and a cloud of feathers, into the half-open door, into the hardly open boot, trying desperately to stop the ones already inside, who do not want to go for a drive, from getting out. It takes a fair time. Lots of people find they are not too busy to watch and offer sardonic advice. And on the way home (it is a warm day), you have the windows shut for obvious reasons, and the smell gets richer and richer, and every so often a passer-by is startled to see a car approaching with a duck looking through its windscreen. Those ducks were eaten pretty soon.

We had ducks too, when the children grew up and could be given chores. They lived on the river at the bottom of the garden, in a shed made out of one of the old privies. Our relationship was always an uneasy one. Mostly, the ducks were given the run of the garden, and from time to time terrorised the labrador, now elderly and stiff, when they got bored. Mostly they behaved themselves. But every so often Griselda,

Out of Reach

or Jemima, would decide to have a proper nest, and would disappear up the river to some impossible haunt to lay a clutch of sterile eggs. Every so often, Griselda seemed to be able to attract a drake, usually a mallard, but it never came to much: the pair looked rather like a Donald McGill wife with apologetic husband. On one notable occasion a lame Muscovy of ancient days and unknown origins, with a beak that looked as if it had an eruption of grog-blossoms, appeared as the new, and ineffective, Lothario. So, after all these escapades, bending with the wind, we got Griselda a drake, which unfortunately made the problem more frequent - even though she was getting to be a lady of advanced age. She became eccentric in the extreme: she would disappear to her hideout, which we eventually found was nearly a quarter of a mile away, to sit her clutch, and then arrive at six in the morning with a great flurry of paddles and wings, quacking wildly under our window to be fed, gobbling her food, and then steaming off upstream to get back before the eggs got cold - they often did. She is the only duck I have come across who ignored the seasons in her mating: she arrived one December morning, with twelve yellow ducklings behind her. (That lot did not survive, despite penning them and looking after them: after losing two a day, morning and evening, for four days, I caught the culprit one morning - next door's cat, eating them like lollipops.)

Ducks are canny things. The ducklings would eat from our hands until the morning, when they were about ten weeks old, on which I had decided with Jenny to kill them. Then they would not come near the place. Some were so elusive we eventually had to shoot them with a .22, and wade into the river to pick them up. And then there was the winter when the ducks decided to move upriver, and while they were up there, the river froze solid, making return impossible. How to feed them? So Justin and I, thigh-booted - for the ice was unreliable - carrying landing nets, moved up the river seeking them. We found them, tucked under a piece of ivy-covered corrugated iron. With difficulty, we winkled them out, and then made our way back to the house along the lane.

Out of Reach

Unfortunately, there were people about, who for years after embroidered the story of the two of us, each with a duck under each arm, in waders, with nets, walking through the village. That story caused justified merriment, just as did the time when I had to catch the drake and rugby-tackled him in the river. There are always people who see the moments we ourselves would rather forget.

We had hens for years: everyone did. Just as during the war, they were waste converters, a way of squeezing just that bit more out of a small income. They fed on our scraps, they foraged on the riverbank, they were given gourmet meals of meal and mash and chopped (wormy) mushrooms to see if the mushrooms, having passed through their gut, would be triggered into growing in their pen (yes). It became a monthly ritual to go to the corn merchant and get Peter, one eye blue and one eye hazel, tiny as a leprechaun, to weigh out some layer's meal for us and crack his joke. They rewarded us with eggs such as I have never eaten since. Broody, they hatched out ducks - for ducks are unreliable mothers - and they had the henny equivalent of breakdowns when these strange chicks took to the water. One year, one hen hatched a partridge egg I had found; the partridge chick was just bite-size for next door's cat. Feeding them came to be the children's job before school, along with walking the dog and mucking out the horse - a hard training, but one that teaches that responsibilities don't go away, that the new pet or pastime of summer also needs care and love in the lashing rain of winter.

I don't think the children had the affection for the hens and their pensive churckling that I came to have. The first lot, of course, they treated as pets, and had a tearful funeral for the bones after they realised who had been the Christmas dinner they had just enjoyed. (After that, the hens still has names, but ones like Roast, Fried, Boiled.) They tested to see

Out of Reach

whether hens could swim by making them fly over the river. (I had been puzzled by why the hens were often so wet until I caught them at it.) They ruined the temper of one cockerel by spraying him with the garden hose, which he hated (who can blame him?) so that any human being was attacked on sight. He met his end after he took things too far one hot day when, shirtless, I was giving the hens their afternoon feed. No warning, but suddenly there he was, both spurs buried in my dorsal muscles. No bird was ever despatched more quickly, or eaten with less regret. It is an unjust world.

Every so often we needed a new cockerel. Behind Ida's farm, in a yard that opened out onto the henny equivalent of the fields of Paradise, the hens had multiplied exceedingly. They scratched in the debris that fell from the ventilator of the corn drier, they feasted on the apples and cherries in season, they raided the spillings of corn from the seed drill or the combine or the elevator. In addition, Ida fed them. They grew luxuriant and fat, and a great nation, and her son was always trying to get rid of the surplus. Ten cocks crowing at once early on a summer morning can be less than soothing. We were invited to help ourselves.

Those birds were athletic. They did not try to fly: they ran, with longer legs and lighter-built bodies than most of their race - which should have warned us, if we had been alert. In the end, three of us got an indignant young cockerel in the corner of a shed, under a hay rack where he could not fly out. We bundled him into a box, and took him back home. We introduced him to his new harem, point-of-lay birds from market, and hoped all would be well. First rearranging his leggy dignity, he then crowed: and we thought then we might have made a mistake, for he cried with an exceeding great voice. The expectant maidens watched, huddled together in a corner. Poor things, they had had no sort of a life up to then: we found they had been intended for the concentration

Out of Reach

camps of a battery farm, and had been debeaked so that they could never peck with the attentive accuracy of other hens. We felt, indeed, we had rescued them from a fate worse than death. But if hens can have looks on their faces, those hens disagreed with us as they looked at this strange world, and this strange beast at the opposite side of the pen we left them to it and went to wash the scratches that were beginning to come up into weals.

When we came back, two hens were being repeatedly convinced that they were no longer maidens. A third was selling her virtue dearly, and had quite a turn of speed. All seemed to be well, and by evening they were feeding together reasonably happily, even if the debeaked ones found more difficulty in picking food up.

Their progeny were extraordinary. The genes of that young cock must have been a rare mixture. Some of the new generation had rose combs, some feathers on their feet, some were tall and leggy, others short and stout. Some were black, some grey. some brown. And they were all sizes. And the leggy cockerel got sharper-tempered day by day. John looked at them over the wire. ''Course, those black ones are just like those old Black Minorcas', he said thoughtfully. He was going hack a long way, past generations of hens in his life, back to the time when cock fighting was common in the remoter parts of the parish. And true enough: those chickens in that yard to this day betray their fighting ancestry the cocks square up to each other with a quickness and agility which makes a couple of sparring cock pheasants, who are lively enough, look like a battle of tortoises.

The cock, in the end, had to go: we had not the heart to kill him. He needed more scope for his ambitions, so we caught him one night as he roosted - indignant still - and took him back where he came from. And set him free. His wives did not mourn him. One, indeed, harassed beyond endurance, had scuttled into a crevice behind the stable and, unable to turn round, and too stupid to go into reverse, had died with her face to the wall.

Out of Reach

Of course, the later hens got names willy-nilly. Little Tid, half the size she should have been, busy all day long, who developed a limp in extreme old age. A night of terrible frost killed her. Or Cottonsocks, so-called because way back in her ancestry some bantam forebear had had feathered feet. Her grey, depressed little form was accident prone: it was Cottonsocks who trod on her eggs, it was Cottonsocks on whose neck the automatic feeder would slowly descend until she was too late to withdraw her head, it was Cottonsocks who held irresistible and incessant charms for a cock (he did not last long) which seemed to have the avian equivalent of satyriasis. Little Antonia, noticing these goings on, reported to us that the cock was saying, 'If you don't lay an egg for my tea, I'll sit on you.' Near enough, I suppose; but Cottonsocks suddenly became plump and fat when that cock got his come-uppance.

And then there were the geese. This was going to be the next moneymaker: geese made a good price as dressed birds (why do we not say undressed?) each Christmas, and rearing them ourselves would provide not only our own dinner but also a cash return from the sale of the others. We did not have enough land to keep them on ourselves, so we arranged to put them in Colin's orchard in return for fattening one for him for Christmas. A weekend was spent fencing in a sizeable plot that gave onto the river, and the next Wednesday off we went to Bury to buy some goslings. Getting them back was no picnic, for even when young they are powerful birds and know how to protest. Once upon a time we would have walked them home, as once thousands of them walked every year to the London markets from Norfolk and Suffolk -

Out of Reach

before rapid transport and refrigeration, they had to be killed as near the point of consumption as possible. How did their feet manage on the cruel flinty roads of this part of the world, I wondered: and Seth had the answer, which I did not believe. I found out, long after he was dead, that he was right. You drove your geese through a shallow puddle of wet tar, and then through sand; and again, and again. Just about all you did not do was put hobnails on them. Those geese probably had feet like rigid platforms to get them to their destined tables.

Our eight very soon settled down, to their satisfaction at least: summer's lease, a temporary paradise. They were just at the stage when their adult feathers had all but displaced the last relics of down - the last down to disappear seems to be on the head, and one, which for weeks had a fringe of white down round his smooth pate, rapidly got the name of a frequent visitor similarly endowed. It was difficult remembering not to call the bird by its name when he was around. The little flock soon found their way onto the river, where they terrorised the family of swans. They clamoured whenever a gate was opened or a voice heard within a hundred yards. They jostled up to the fence when Jenny went to feed them of a morning and evening, their beaks wide, sticking their tongues out and staring with their scabious-blue eyes until their courage failed them. Jenny never came to love them: they deposited green offerings all over the place, they honked and hissed when things did not please them, and eventually, intelligent creatures, they found that they could have a jolly excursion if they went along the river, paddled out onto the hythe, and goose-stepped through the village eating people's gardens as they went. Jenny was constantly disturbed by knocks on the door, and, 'Mrs M, your geese are out again.' And there and then she had to stop what she was doing, pick up a pan and a spoon, go and find which garden they were wrecking, or which road they were blocking - for they would not move for traffic - and then lead them home beating the pan, with the eight white figures in line-astern. Small wonder that remarks about little goose-girls did not go down well.

Out of Reach

The allotment was one of a number on seventeen acres set aside, reserved for the poor, under the 1802 Enclosure Act for the parish. Those poor had lost their commoners' rights of turbary, messuage and fowling when the fen was enclosed and drained by the bands of Adventurers who had the capital to generate a lot of wealth for themselves. In bad times, those common rights had made the difference between surviving and feeding and warming a family, and not doing so; in better times, they allowed a landless man to keep a few sheep, a few geese, perhaps a cow and a pig - to give him and his family some independence and dignity. The acreage set aside for the allotments under the Enclosure Act was calculated, not ungenerously, on the number of inhabitants at that time, and a half-acre plot of good land was sufficient to make a worthwhile contribution to the feeding of a large family. But no provision was made for animals, or for the problem of young people growing up and wanting, needing, their own space and the wherewithal to feed themselves. The Enclosure Acts accelerated the process whereby the English peasant lost his independence and became a paid labourer, at the mercy of the market. They also helped to push a lot of folk out of the countryside, where some sort of a living might be had, into the growing towns. Undoubtedly the supply of food for the generality of the population was increased, and undoubtedly improvements in agriculture happened which would have been impossible without the physical concentration of land under the control of people with investment capital. But the human cost in the countryside was huge.

The allotments were (and are) good land, but heavy: in winter like glue, impossible to dig; in summer, if trodden too much, like concrete. But the soil yields well, and has done for thousands of years. The side of the hill bears the marks of Iron-Age grain storage pits; the soil is full of pottery fragments, and pieces of the clay pipes men smoked until the

Out of Reach

First World War. Their backs before mine bent to that stiff land, their hands cracked with its alkaline bite. It was an eerie moment when, straightening up from weeding a row of onions, my eye caught a glint in the disturbed soil: a neolithic arrowhead. Who was that man who had hunted over that land, as I hunted in his place the rabbits and pheasants he had never known, who would, like those who followed him, have grown into an hoop with the labouring of that soil? As I held it my hand - I have it still - suddenly forty centuries were watching: and judging my stewardship.

There was ample room for a cash crop as well as vegetables. We tried sowing barley broadcast in the old way and made a mess of it (as we were told we would); we tried harnessing ourselves to a single-furrow seed drill of nineteenth-century vintage and drilling it, which was a little better, but incredibly slow. In the end we borrowed or hired plough and tractor, seed drill and harvester, and as Justin got older this came to be his hobby, job, and income. Years later, long after Justin had grown to be powerful enough to work alongside me, just before he left home, we carted a load of our own barley to the corn merchant.

The man tested the sample, pursed his lips, and said, 'Good malting barley, that. What sort of price are you looking for?'

I think that was one of the proudest moments of my life, and I tried not to show it. I glanced at Justin, and said, casually, as if I really could not care, and would as soon go somewhere else (there was nowhere), 'Oh, about hundred and twenty.'

He pursed his lips again, and shook his head. 'Give you hundred and ten.'

'Say hundred and fifteen,' I heard myself saying, and caught Justin's astonished eye again.

'Done,' the man said.

I swanked about that barley for a long time, for, all unwitting, I had got the best price in the village. I could, at last, claim to have done everything in that village as well as anyone else.

Out of Reach

Almost the first word Justin spoke had been 'tacter'. His first Dinky Toy was a model Fordson Major, which clicked when you ran it along the ground, and had a driver you could take out of the cab. His earliest heroes were those who drove tractors. And later, some of the farmers who were in a very small way welcomed the help of a strong and willing lad - whom they did not have to pay. Justin had no trouble finding someone who would let him learn to drive a tractor, and handle machinery. Don was only too glad to have help, and large, slow Don and quick little Justin would go off to the yard in their gumboots and flat caps (Justin insisted on having one, to go with the part) for all the world like Pooh and Piglet.

The village said of Don that he had only two speeds, dead slow and stop, and he was indeed deliberate, methodical and patient with his antiquated machinery, which was all he could afford. There were many excuses for not hurrying: the land was either too wet or too dry, or the cutter-bar had broken, or the spreader needed greasing. But some training in being patient was no bad thing for a young lad in a hurry; and being trusted on his own with machinery to do a big job came soon enough. Ploughing alone down the fen, and seeing a big dog-fox curled up asleep in a sunny ditch, or sweet oily whiffs of the hot engine on the wind on a day of scudding clouds - he filled up his sensibility soon enough, and laid in a store of memories of first responsibilities, as I can still smell the engine-room and fish-hold of the trawlers I worked on as a youth.

Don's gruff pleasure in some company in a lonely job did not stop him giving Justin a hard time, sometimes. A lost ploughshare, which can happen to anyone - and it was nearly worn away anyway - drew the rebuke, 'Always in too much of a bloody 'urry.' He kept the boy working, often at jobs that were at the limit of his growing strength. In return, Justin had

Out of Reach

the loan, when needed, of the tractor, and the plough, and the hay cutter, and the trailer - without them, working our allotment would have been much more difficult. And the boy got to draw a straight furrow, to take a pride in well-tilled earth. One memory of this period seems so significant, I do not know why - as if of a rite of passage seen to be completed. Jenny and I walked down to the land to see how Justin was getting on with the job, and there was his tractor followed by one of the loveliest of sights, the first bubbling flock of winter gulls delicately dibbling at the fresh chocolate furrows, which shone as the light caught them, and the noise of the gulls' brawling carried on the wind above the chug of the engine.

I once enthused, naively, about the dignity of work, the beauty of simple tasks well done, to Toby, who in his youth had been a horseman on one of the farms, up at five, readying the horses for the daily labour of the fields, and rubbing them down at three at the end of their toil. In particular, I talked about the pride a man took in drawing a straight furrow, setting out his field in stetches with the precision of a draughtsman. I got a very funny sidelong look; and then the slow reply,

'Cutting a straight furrow was just about all you had that you could take a pride in then, mate.'

I felt about ten inches tall; I had fallen into the intellectual's perennial snare, of romanticising work, of forgetting the wet, cold feet, the smell of soaked wool, the cracked hands, the aching back - and forgotten the sheer plod of privation, poverty and pain that made the plough-down-sillion shine. Toby bore no grudge, but others might well have done.

Romantic pastoral life was very far from Don's yard. The nettles grew straight and tall each summer, except where diesel spills had soaked the soil. Where there were no nettles, tall thistles 'to the ragged infant threatened war'. In the nettles, somewhere, was the equipment you wanted. First find it ('Pair o' tin trousers yew need to git that', Seth used to say, scathingly). Then cut it out; then grease its rust; then hitch it up to the tractor. Grunts and swears rather than

Out of Reach

pastoral airs punctuated the working day, and nobody got off lightly.

Overheard one summer morning, as the two of them were trying to manhandle a mass of rusty iron into place on the hydraulic arms of the tractor: 'Y're as much use as a fart in a bucket: cop hold o' that, and keep hold this time.' They worked happily together most of the time, nevertheless, until the time came for Justin to turn to his own world and leave those of others behind in the long colonnades of memory.

Don's lugubriousness was funereal. Yet his solemnity was occasionally punctuated, not removed, by smiles that started in his big grey eyes and spread down his large, egg-shaped face, to his heavy jowls: rarely, a deep laugh accompanied by a pushing back of his cap from his bald pate, revealing an acreage of shiny white marked off at the line where his cap habitually settled from a face tilled and bronzed by sun and weather. Uncommunicative as he was we nevertheless suspected rare moments of passion; what was the reason for suddenly presenting newcomer Maggie with a bunch of rhubarb, and showing her, on his neck, the great scar got in a near-fatal shotgun accident? (He had never told us about it.) For all his life, his sister did his washing, and looked after him and their old Dad in their little house up the street. So it was something of a sensation to find, when old Stan died, that Don had had, for years, a lady friend, whom no one had ever seen, and whose existence nobody had suspected. He moved in with her in a village several miles away, and he leaves our story.

When Antonia reached her teens, the pressures to have a pony became considerable, and grandparents conspired to make pressure irresistible and purchase possible. So, a flurry of building activity as we added a stable, with hayloft and tack-room, to the range of buildings in the garden, in order to accommodate the new arrival. (Nothing ever rises as slowly

Out of Reach

as a wall you build yourself.) Then the horse arrived: a big-boned, cobby fellow of uncertain energy and hard mouth, cynical as only ex-riding-school horses can be. As good as gold when we had seen him in the school, now he was on his own his true colours came out; lazy, casual, slovenly, stubborn. He was the making of Antonia. One afternoon his temper, never very reliable, boiled over, and he would not be ridden. He bucked her off, and she got on again. And again; and again. Her hot little face got redder and redder, her clothes muddier and muddier, but she was determined to beat him. And in the end, she did; it was a turning point in her life, I think, when that horse finally did move quietly out into the road, and arch his neck into a trot, and trot round the corner out of sight of his luxurious stable. The real battle had been won inside Antonia, bruised, stiff for days, and angry. We did not speak of it, but we all knew, and knew we all knew, that an important bit of growing up had been done.

Mariner won little affection, not surprisingly. We traded him on quite soon for another beast, the by-blow, so it was said and so it looked, of an Arab stallion with a Welsh mare. Robbie became a part of the family, whose colds were treated with hot mashes, whose aches and pains were discussed at table endlessly, whose face my 85-year-old mother washed when the flies bothered it on hot days. Robbie had people sit with him when he was ill. Robbie followed me round the garden like a dog, and learnt to open his gate and pick apples off the trees. Robbie thought it a great game to play catch-as-catch-can round the beehives, and creep up behind the hens scratching in his straw and blow on them. And Robbie loved to look at himself in shop windows, and used to stop without asking at a pub because he loved his pint of lager and black. Robbie was a modest horse, who would only defecate in a corner of his stable. But Robbie needed feeding - and feeding, and feeding.

So we began to make hay on the drove-ways each June. Nobody stopped us; but 25 years earlier the right to cut the drove-ways had been auctioned each May in the pub in the next village: Albert told me the going rate was usually half-a-

Out of Reach

crown. Now nobody wanted the hay, for there were few animals, and the sheep that had grazed this land since the Romans were remembered only in the odd place name, or in a pair of hand shears hanging rusting on a wall. It was a grand sward: sweet and full of fescue and clover, and as it dried we four cast it into windrows where it whitened into ripeness, and then carted it home smelling like the breath of a calf.

Those were some of the golden days, when we hurrahed in harvest - all of us fit, and able to work hard together, keeping pace for pace, getting into the almost balletic rhythm that Seth described the gang of mowers maintaining as they moved across a field in echelon laying the swathes behind them. Or bringing home a brimming trailer-load of hay on a June afternoon, with me driving the tractor, and Antonia and Justin aloft, lying back full length in the most luxurious of beds. Yet my memory filters out the dash home from work and school to turn the hay, the worry about the weather holding, the anxiety with which we watched a big cumulus cloud sailing up from the west.

We all learned to manage a horse - though some were more optimistic than others. I learned, too, that the world not only looks, but is, different from the back of a horse. It is not simply a question of point of view, or even the fact that you think like a horse, anticipating hazards and terrors before it does; it is not, either, the fact that wildlife takes far less notice of you on four feet than on two. More subtly, it is about power, and authority, I think.

I remember riding over to the next village on Mariner, the first horse, to see a friend. I turned off the road, and the hooves' note changed as Mariner trotted down the little lane, over the large flints, and into the farmyard where John was working. He straightened up as he heard the hoofs, and wiped his hands on his sacking apron. We stopped, and John and I began to chat, Mariner moving gently every so often, flicking a fly away from his ear, shuddering his withers, or lifting and lowering his ugly head. Suddenly, sitting there, I sensed that my relationship with John had changed: he was looking up, I down; I had the advantage of the light and

Out of Reach

height. I suddenly guessed at the old authority of the man on a horse over the man on foot, the dominance of the rider, the knight, over the footman, the old hierarchical order that had in part made these villages of England the way they were, physically and socially. The Vicar's wife striking the boy who one day would be churchwarden and Chairman of the Parish Council across the face with a riding crop; the wanton trooper riding by, the dragoon at Peterloo; the Norman knight amid the Saxon peasantry. And John picked up my thought: he began to talk about the old squire, who used to ride round to see all was well in the village 'on his old horse, just like you. Hearing those hoofs, they brought back Memories, they did.'

An odd moment, not altogether pleasant, though its clarity in memory has golden edges. Something stirred deep in the shadows of my mind, which I did not recognise, and did not wholly like. Musing later, as Mariner reluctantly cantered home, I thought I knew what it was: the desire for sheer, unfocused power. Or it may have been something odder, an unconscious matching of that moment to the forgotten daydreams of a child's mind, filled with a heroic, romantic view of a world where swords were as usual as walking sticks, and Lochinvar, and Joris, and Dick Turpin - the narrative design on the brown jug on my grandmother's cupboard! - rode furiously out of the west, to Aix, to York... I do not know.

That first horse, of course, humiliated us more successfully than he did Antonia. Jenny had to do a good deal for him when I was away, and that included taking him the quarter mile to the grazing we had rented for him. He shared the field with Robbie (whom we eventually bought, once he settled down a bit), with showy little Dixie, and with fat George. Who knows how they got on? There were clearly tensions from time to time. But those four horses were full of cunning.

Out of Reach

Normally, there was no trouble; but one day Jenny sets off to take Mariner, dancing up and down at the end of a lead rein, down to his grazing. She gets him down to the gate, and the other three are standing round it waiting. She undoes the gate. Mariner jumps up, because gates are terribly frightening things. Robbie pushes forward, pushes the gate open, and Jenny loses hold of both gate and Mariner. Dixie gives a leer, and trots out after Robbie. George thinks for a moment and walks out too. And the four of them begin to have the best party of their lives.

There is not a thing Jenny can do. To attempt to catch any one is impossible in the state of excitement they are in. They have jumped the ditch - or, rather, three of them have and George has scrambled over it - and are guzzling Albert's sugar beet. She cautiously approaches, but Mariner is up with his heels and off to another part of the field, followed by the others. But, gradually, they calm down under the influence of the unaccustomed food, and a neighbour comes along, and he and Jenny manage, in the end, to get them back into the field. And now she wonders what Albert will say, and she has to pass his farm on the way back.

Albert, who has seen it all, says nothing. But 'Mrs Moseley and her rodeo' took a lot of living down. I heard many versions of the story, and it lost nothing in the telling.

You cannot feed a horse only on hay, so we began to think of cutting out one stage in the process whereby we grew on our allotment a crop to sell, and then bought feed with the money. Why not grow feed directly on allotment? Now the first horse had a passion for swedes, and so, when Robbie came, we thought a few rows of swedes would be useful. We grew a furlong of swedes, which is a lot, and they yielded magnificently - nearly a ton. But Robbie took one bite of the first, and spat it out: he did not like swedes any more than Tigger liked haycorns. We were left with a lot of swedes, and

Out of Reach

we ate them, we gave them as presents when we went on visits, we offered them to visitors, we even tried to find a recipe for swede wine. Never since have I been able to grow swedes of such sweet rotundity, such bravura magnificence.

The story of our swedes was another thing that kept the pub happy on Sunday mornings. If I had it all to do again, I would know what I was doing.

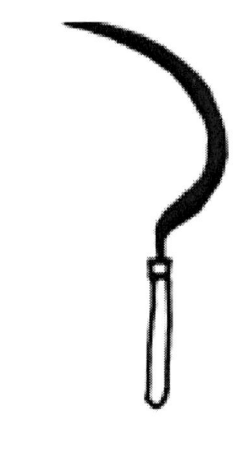

Chapter Twelve

Seth looked as tough as a tree root, but he had 'engine trouble'. His heart had been weakening for years, and he had been warned that he could drop dead at any time. He made no secret of this, but not in any morbid way - more as a sort of joke. Mother-in-law, on a later visit, long after she had got used to us having friends like Seth, listened wide-eyed as Seth, having invited himself in for a chat as we were finishing lunch, came out cheerfully with his prognosis of imminent doom. When he stopped, waiting for the embarrassed reaction he loved to play with, she said, breathlessly, 'But hasn't it made you recognise the importance of the spiritual side of life?'

He had not expected that; and gave her a sly look: 'Doctor says I've not to drink.'

He did not let his heart stop him doing anything he wanted to. He still went off down the fen alone for hours on end, and I have wondered since how Mrs Seth must have felt about that. Hardly able to walk herself, she would have had no idea where to tell others to look for him. A brave woman:

Out of Reach

I have seen the pain in her black eyes and in the pucker round her toothless mouth, but she knew it was useless to try and stop 'the old devil'. He still went off with his gun; he still set off on his bicycle with his felling axe, and cross-cut saw, wrapped in sacking, and a bag of wedges and a beetle, to split up a bog-oak someone had ploughed out and given him. (I still have his wedges, and beetle, and saw.)

And then there came the summer when he was told a little more firmly than usual to take things easy. So he decided to take up fishing: nice quiet sport, just sitting on a bank watching a float, the doctor thought. But he did not know Seth. First he got a rod - an old one of my father's. Then he found a place to fish, where there was deep water, just where the barges used to swing round. But there was far too much weed in that water for Seth. And there I found him one morning, standing in a borrowed punt, swinging his second-best scythe a yard under water to cut the reeds and weeds, and then raking the debris aboard. I offered to take over, and my young muscles were screaming in protest in a matter of minutes. But I was not allowed to stop until Seth had his patch of weed-free water to fish in. He tried it - twice. And then decided he didn't like fishing. 'Too slow, mate.'

He gave me a couple of old scythe blades, with their tacks and grass-nails and leather wedges to fit to a snaithe. He made me one out of a piece of ash, grudgingly: I was firmly told that I ought to do this myself. In his day, I was reminded, men chose a likely looking branch or stem and trained it for a couple of growing years to a curve to fit their stance and swing: the sort of thing that I would have done had I had a proper education. But I hadn't got a stance or a swing. And he stood over me in front of the house while I hacked some grass - where everyone could see. 'Learning him to use a scythe, eh, Seth?' and a grin, as people went past. And my back ached after ten minutes, and the sweat streamed into my

Out of Reach

eyes, and Seth carried on saying, 'Keep her heel down', and relating how he had in his prime cut each day two acres of wheat or four acres of barley - and then, without a word, took the scythe from me, swung it easily over the sward, and left an immaculate swathe behind him. Then gave it me back. 'Not bad for an old 'un.' A favourite phrase: he used it often. Oddly, I found myself using it the other day. Without irony.

He could never leave things alone - they could always be made better. He went behind my lawnmower cutting grass with his scythe to prove it did a better job. (Lots of grass around, but arguable.) We went away on a rare holiday, and came back to find one part of the lawn six inches high, and the other like a cut hayfield. Seth had had the scythe out, and told us he would have done the lot if someone had not seen him and chaffed him with doing other people a favour. I bought a pointing trowel, which Seth immediately purloined, and returned with the blade shortened and the point more rounded. I can't see why it should do a better job, but I use it still. My father's saw he took away to sharpen, knocked all the teeth off it, and re-cut them all with a triangular file. Pincers always had their handles lengthened with bits of pipe, so that they would chew through far thicker things than any pincer was ever meant to. His house was immaculate, his yard impeccable, and the weeds kept their heads down on his land. A hard companion for the sloppy casualness of my youth, but a good one.

An autumn came when the weather worsened early, and we had not got all the wood in off the fen for winter firing. One Saturday, a day of low, scudding cloud, the wind thinking about rain, we went off with ropes and tractor and trailer to

Out of Reach

get the wood he had been splitting - about two tons of it. The two of us loaded the stuff onto the trailer, and in the gathering dusk I started roping it on. It took me a minute or so to realise that Seth was not telling me I was doing it wrong: he was hunched up, grey, against the muddy wheel. Somehow, I got him aboard - not into the cab, for those old tractors had none, but onto the load of wood - and put a rope round him to give him some support. It was rapidly growing dark, we were two miles from home, and the rain was at last beginning to settle in. Tractors are not fast things, nor if they had been could that one have been driven fast over the fen track. I got its revs up as far as I dared, and belted up the fen towards the distant lights of the village; I kept on looking back at the hunched figure jerkily silhouetted against the failing remains of light in the west.

We were in time, just. I drove the tractor straight into his yard, right up to the back door, and got him down. Jenny had seen the lights, and guessed from the screaming engine that something was wrong. A quick glance sent her off to ring the ambulance. Seth, by the time they came, had recovered sufficiently to tell me off for driving too fast, bark at Mrs Seth for making a fuss, and tell Jenny she was looking pretty as a picture. The ambulance went up the street with him protesting inside: and that was the time he made them go back for his false teeth. One ambulance man was heard to say, 'We've got a right awkward old bugger here.' If only they knew. . .

He recovered, and came back smelling of hospital: it took a week or to for him to get his own, slightly musty, smell, compound of oak smoke and old clothes, back again. He never stopped teasing me about that drive, and he continued to do his own jobs and tell everybody else how to do theirs. He still came over to supervise what I was doing. And Christmas time came, and I was putting in a new floor. Jenny was standing with Seth, watching, and he was in the middle of one of his interminable and unspeakable stories. And then, while my saw (Seth had just sharpened it) snored in the wood, he suddenly stopped. Mid-sentence. And fell.

Out of Reach

We got him to a chair, but though I tried mouth-to-mouth resuscitation and cardiac massage, neither of us needed to be told by the doctor when he came that we were wasting our time. It had been all too plain from the moment we had picked him up.

We carried him across the street, in the frost, on an old door we had taken out. I turned it over so that the nails on which coats used to hang should not hurt him. Silly. Mrs Seth received him quietly, without a cry: she had been expecting this for years, but had hoped, without much hope, that he would die with her - the only ambition she had left from the days of their youth together. Hints from Seth, and her, suggested those days had been stormy, passionate, quarrelsome: but no-one will ever know the truth of their version of their lives. I helped her unlace his boots when we had laid him on the bed. It was then she cried, briefly. And then I left him to Jenny and Mrs Seth, and went to get Tilly Bowyer and to ring his son.

His old clock, wood painted to look like marble, ticked in my college room for years, and sits, now no longer ticking, where I see it every day. 'Ticker trouble'. He was our first brush with death - there have been others since - and the first is always the one that suddenly opens the shutters of the mind. The urgency of life: Seth knew it well. And after the fitful fever, he seemed to sleep well. Jenny, that night, said a strange thing - we were very young: 'Do you know, I found I envied him.'

Little Harold Sennett, all big belly, little legs in black gumboots, little black eyes deep-set either side of his big beak nose; quick little eyes, darting like those of the little mouse I disturbed having a busy little feed in my corn bin. Too-big cap set skew-whiff on a head for all I ever knew devoid of hair. Little breathless Harold, talking telegraphically, allusively (to what?), always in a hurry, in his little round-

Out of Reach

bonneted Morris Minor van, open the door, hop out, trot trot trot. Never in too much hurry not to talk though; still an eye for a pretty face (not so pretty, doesn't matter) still the randy old devil we glimpse in the scattered leaves of his unconnected anecdotes, unplaced in time.

Good friend to Seth: knew he poached, didn't mind, do the same himself given half a chance - often does in the Nature Reserve - lets him have some peats, take what you want, takes all Seth's junk away when Seth dies (and gets Seth's best gun: deserves it).

Little Harold Sennett, finding useful things all over just where people have dropped them - look what I've got in my car - my knife - use it a lot - just found it lying about. (The knife he has carried around for years is a most beautiful polished neolithic axehead, sharp and keen. Its first owner would recognise its present one: a hunter, a predator, alert, busy.)

He was one of the three who wept openly at Seth' funeral. Afterwards, the memory of that life was all our different lives had in common, and it made us feel we ought to talk when we bumped into each other, though we never once referred to it. There was little to say.

Seth's life had been running out while Justin was very young, and he never saw him grow up to have his own shadow. Yet as the boy grew up into a world where Seth and his stories were a memory for Jenny and me, it was as if the place itself imposed on him a way of being that often made us think how much pleasure Seth might have taken in seeing him mature - a way of being that I had acquired, but which to Justin was natural as breathing. The economical use, and reuse, of what had been found, often abandoned by someone else; the quietness, and keen eye, that could sit in a ditch and have baby rabbits playing at the end of the gun barrels, or notice a kingfisher's ultramarine lightning cutting the brilliance of the

Out of Reach

morning. A secret life I envied: a countryman to his finger tips. ... .

He went away, of course, as was right, taking with him a view of the village wholly closed to Jenny and me with our different stories. We overlapped in the unsayable, in places and things. The last evening before he left to sail North for a season to where the brash ice growls along the side of the boat in the fog and snow buntings nest on the storm beach, the four of us walked down to the allotment as the June sun was sinking over the fen. We did not say much, for there was too much to say. This, like our arrival when there had just been two of us, was a rite of passage: and among the neat rows of our vegetables, or in the early ears of our wheat, half of me - the 'natural heart' - was self-ironically expecting to see a sheepfold. But the bathetic always intrudes, thank goodness. Parked at the edge of our land was a car, the radio on, a couple self-absorbed inside, a naked foot thrust through the open window (it was a very little car). The comedy broke the ice, and we left them to it, sure they were not going to muck up our standing corn. We picked a few onions for luck, turned for home and the journey he had to make without us.

But it was sometime before he left to go up to Cambridge that the climactic moment came, where his two lives, the one he had from the place and what it had been, and the one he had from us, intersected, as they perhaps never will again. He acted regularly as acolyte on the altar at the parish church, and the Vicar and everyone else relied on him, even, perhaps, thinking that here was a future priest. No-one could have looked more saintly.

Came one Christmas Eve, and Justin had been out with his gun all afternoon. He came home late, glowing with the cold, and quietly pleased about something. We wondered if he had once again been giving the horse a totally superfluous grooming with a girl from the next village. But he kept quiet, until it was nearly time to go to the midnight service. For the first time, a hint of embarrassment. Could we, perhaps, go a little early? That girl, perhaps, we think. So Justin gets into his cassock, and off we go. As soon as we arrive, he disappears into the night. And just as the first worshippers are beginning to straggle up the street to the steps up to the church, he returns, with something bulky under his cassock. 'Here, Dad, take these, and put them in the car.'

Two fine cock pheasants. I take them, and he disappears without a word. All through the service I watch this angelic youth in amice and alb with a sort of awe, and my mind not on my devotions at all. Later, the story comes out: the birds were shot on the land of the churchwarden and JP who has just been talking to us after the service, saying what a fine young man the boy is turning into. He could not bring them home because he was on his bike, and had no bag. So he hid them behind a tombstone, to pick them up safely later.

Seth would have been proud of him, for, indirectly, he had more than a small share in the way he grew. I am not altogether sure even now how I felt about those pheasants. But they ate well. And my son had passed my farthest North.

No landfall without departures. Justin leaving for the Arctic, Antonia leaving for Scotland, started when they first began the toddling exploration of the hugeness of their garden, and then a whole country of which they were natives, but in which we were adopted. Their stories of this place are unknowable to me, just as Jenny's is. For Antonia, the woodshed will always be a place where Looie lived, a child of the mind for a solitary child to play with. In their world trees that, for me, are grown-out fence posts, for them held dens in their pollarded crowns, cupping memories of secret conclaves of high import with their friends. (Some most unsuitable. . . .) The village school, where long years ago I had served as Manager, for them is not a place as it is for Jenny and me, but central memory, filled with the cabbala of children's games and unintended trauma.

A wise man - he who preached at Colin's funeral, and was to assist at Antonia's wedding - once rebuked me as I was about to insist that an idle, adolescent Antonia stop sitting on the bridge swinging her legs over the water and get on with some work: 'Leave her: she is filling up her sensibility.'

They grew in our shade, but had to move out of our shadow; we had to let go. And as their moorings slackened, as they turned and drew close to their own worlds, we understood, for the first time, the loss - and the uneasy pride - our own parents must have felt, the gradual being written-out from a story they had helped to write. But it was too late to signal to them we had understood, for they were dropping below the horizon.

Not so long ago, on a summer evening, several men would be down on the allotments working, tending the vegetables, and the rows of stocks, and sweet Williams, and chrysanthemums. The number of people who work the allotments as they used to be worked has now come down to one: myself. Now a summer evening is marked not so much by people working in their gardens or allotments and all too glad to straighten up for a chat, as by the changing, multi-coloured flicker that comes from the uncurtained windows and the wasp noise of all-terrain bikes that carry the young past the silences they never seem to want, or even notice. Old, Master Shallow.

The house now is surrounded by other houses, which have sprouted on the orchard next door, on George's vegetable patch, and across the road where Seth's cottage, walnut tree, and bog-oak sheds once huddled. People come and say how remote, how uncrowded we are - and, sometimes, I catch them looking oddly at our old-fashioned garden, or at our sheds full of useful things that will come in one day, at the

Out of Reach

range of tools hanging on the walls in the workshop. One visitor, who only came once, congratulated us on having a site ideal for redevelopment. I am sure that their new houses are as magical, and their village as entrancing, to the new owners, as ours was to us. But there are some things we can never tell them about so that they will know what we mean.

How can we tell people of what it was like to live in a place of trust, where you never even thought of locking a door? How George, if we were away, would take it upon himself to guard the house from everybody, stalling them with his incomprehensible speech till even those we had invited felt constrained to drive up the street and sit in their cars and wait until one of us appeared. (Where we even went away once for a whole weekend and left the place unlocked, we now use five-lever deadlocks back and front.)

Or the cows: when we first came, after haysel and for the remaining drier months of the year, Ernie's cows used to amble past the house night and morning, wet, shiny muzzles desultorily snatching a mouthful of elm leaves off my trees in summer, or clumsily lumbering over the front grass to guzzle the fermenting apples fallen off Albert's double-grafted tree in the autumn. Their slow progress was punctuated by noisy dollops of muck along the road, muck which I used to shovel up still sweet and steaming, and steep overnight in a bucket of water: the best manure in the world for tomatoes. Later incomers used to write complaining letters about the cows and the mess they caused.

At the rear came Ernie, with his sixteen-year-old daughter Janey, ambling along with their switches of willow, tickling up the stragglers who paused to take a ruminative bite of grass. I can see now the angular rears of the Friesians going up the hill, followed by Janey's most unangular bottom, in its ripped blue jeans, and her gumbooted lope echoing the side-to-side sway of the cows she tended. Then Janey went away from home to work, and the next we saw of her was unrecognisable: a woman of fashion, polished and sharp, wearing clothes that would never see a cowshed, and shoes more ornament than use. Just visiting, and got to get on. Janey is not a

Out of Reach

bad symbol of what has happened to the village she grew up in.

How can I make even my children feel what it was like to go out with the dog before bed each night, whatever the weather, and to walk a mile or two with the great arch of the heavens undimmed by the nauseous yellow glow of street lights? While the dog continued his preoccupied, self-important inspection of the scents and savours of selected tufts of grass, the two of us would walk on, our night vision unimpaired, and hear the quavering alarm of the plover we disturbed, as its more solid darkness momentarily flitted between us and the sky. On a clear night in summer we would test each other on the summer constellations of Pegasus and Delphinus, Lyra and Cygnus. In August we would watch for the Leonid meteor shower, and as the year waned we would welcome the Pleiades, and the earlier rising of great Orion, with the nebula in his sword quite visible, as signs of the coming of winter pleasures. Our eyes are less clear now, and the lesser stars are hidden by sodium light.

Or, coming up the fen alone on a frosty night, the unlit village indistinguishable against the dark eastern sky. My stumbles over plough or wheel-ruts were guided by habit; until, a mile away, I would see a pin-point of light: our kitchen, where Jenny would be starting to cook supper. The first Homely House in the wilderness, the dark at my back. And as I opened the back door, the warmth would simmer out into the night, and melt the rime on my gun barrels. Home is the hunter, to an hour's Mozart on the upright piano while the supper cooked, and next week's suppers were hanging from the hook by the door.

Easy to romanticise: and easy to forget all the game one missed; or the game one wounded, knew one had wounded, and could not find. Easy to forget the weariness, sometimes, the ache in the legs, the tiredness across the shoulders. And memory's values are not always the ones that were. For as we age, we come to see how others saw us - cocky intruders in a place that did not belong to us. We understand now how people looked at us when we came, and cringe with shame at some of the things we said and did - and thought - in all innocence. But it is too late to apologise to the past; there is a journey still before us.

We were, I suppose, like the first raindrops that herald a thunderstorm. We warmed our hands at the very last embers of English country life as the grandparents of the villagers would have recognised it. Soon after us, the deluge: the revolutions of the '60s, especially those connected with the growth of car ownership, transformed the villages of England, and the old patterns of employment disappeared for ever. Where twelve men had been employed on one farm nearby in 1960, by 1990 two had regular work. House prices rocketed, forcing the young and the poor out of the villages, into council houses which the planners all too often stuck insensitively onto the outskirts of villages when they ought to have been integrated as part of a community, not made to look as if they were a separate, second-rate, not quite decent ghetto of their own.

The village is very much richer than it was, it is very much tidier, it has a Community Association and a village magazine. More trees have been planted - though, alas, the suburban ones of cherry and rowan, rather than the useful ones. (Time was when labourers used to set an apple tree in the hedge or along the railway line, every mile or so - grand quenching of thirst in harvest time in this thirsty countryside.) Its population is much younger, and though the school closed years ago, there are hordes of children. But it has a population that works here hardly at all; it is an outlier of the town and its values are town values, its lore the ubiquitous, ephemeral trivialities of television.

Only a year ago one of the big farms - owned now by a pension fund and managed by a professional manager, educated at Cirencester - ran a coach tour the two miles down the fen for interested villagers so they could see what went on on a farm. The growth in mechanisation has meant that the number of people who know the countryside as more than scenery is small; the number of those who know it really well, in minute detail, has dwindled almost to nothing. Even as walkers along footpaths increase dramatically, the men who in the course of their daily labour walked over, or turned over, every inch of every field, have disappeared. The secret life of the fields is more secret than it has ever been, and the community no longer has the organic relationship with its physical surroundings that was inescapable for centuries.

We ourselves were the first signals of the changes - which might explain, perhaps, why some resented us, dimly recognising what, in our innocence, we portended. We are still, I think, strangers in the village for the older ones who remember our youth, divided from those we came to love by education, by memories, by books that stop one sort of understanding as they develop another, and by the act of writing the untrue truth. We are still on the outside looking in. But - ironies of mere time - for the incomers who are now the majority, we are the unknown inhabitants, the 'old village', the observed, the enigmatical. (Some people have even asked our advice.)

For, after us, things accelerated very fast. A cottage would come on the market as an old person died, and it might be bought as a weekend home, for we are within reach of London. Other incomers too began to arrive, upwardly mobile folk, often first-generation graduates, who bought a little house, did a bit to it, then moved on to something bigger and grander, such as this village does not possess. Little bits of Identikit 1970s NW3 were suddenly transplanted to the country, and very few of the slips really took. Some of them simply were not interested in doing so: the village was simply a place, not a community. Some hardly disguised their amused disregard of the values of the countryfolk, and laughed at them behind open doors. Quite suddenly there were children called Emma or Charlotte (or Antonia, or Justin!) playing in the street. And weekenders: one London wife drove her children round in an old runabout during the week and welcomed her husband's limousine on Fridays. It sat beside Ben's tractor on the grass verge. (It was said of that lady that other friends visited during the week, and Ben's elderly mother, who lived opposite and found she had to spend a lot of time upstairs, said they ought to have drawn the curtains.) The village noticed, and quietly, inarticulately, resented.

The only certainty we have is of change. (Antonia coming back from her first term at University, sitting back outside half a rabbit and - though I say it myself - some magnificent leeks, and saying, in the relaxation of satisfied hunger, 'I had not noticed how grey you both were.') Thirty years of high-tech farming have filled the watercourse with nutrients, so that gone is the clear water forested with patches of delicate weed, where, at the bottom of the garden, when we first came, I used to sit and catch perch on little bits of blue cheese. True, the buckets from people's privies are no longer emptied down the bank, and the village has its sewage works on the mediaeval Hythe, where once it was meadowsweet that in season scented the air. But weeds choke the river now, and you cannot see water in summer for the green growth that pancakes across it, strong enough to bear a moorhen. Gone are the glow-worms, that used to light up in the arching grasses on the banks; and the nightingales that used to sing in Coley's meadow sing no more. Would the incomers know what one sounded like? How can I tell them the thrill of hearing it across the darkling fen at midnight? The river proper is now the preserve of an angling club, who stock it, and catch less than the village boys used to with rods cut from the spring hedges.

I have heard the nightingales in the summer, and the darkling thrush in the winter. I have mown a meadow, and seen the glow-worms, and drawn the weightless grace of fish into the bustle of the air. All true enough. But I cannot vouch for the accuracy with which I recall them, whether I am not rolling the sweetness up into one ball, letting the slanting light of literary memory gild the reality with the setting of the suns that saw it. And this happens all the time: I recall sitting

Out of Reach

fishing at the end of the garden, and the little stream being transformed into a river like Arthur Ransome's; and I tried to smoke a pipe too.

A curious, disturbing conversation one morning. We are doing nothing in particular, idling on the Green, and talking to a woman whose white hair we remember as black, whose husband we remember in full, somewhat cantankerous vigour. We have seen her son grow to middle age, and take over his father's business. Suddenly, she lets us glimpse the tensions, how the young man is doing things his way, and how his father cannot reconcile himself to the way the working of the land has changed. And she is in the middle, mother looking both ways, to the son she bore and the man who courted her. And suddenly, I see, in Jenny's face, her understanding.

Albert is old now, and I have only just realised it. He looks very like his father when he talks, and very like his mother when he listens. His memory reaches back well beyond our own, and we are part of it. Talking on the bridge about the old times, he said to us, 'Wor yew here before the war?'. His memory has telescoped a time before we were born into a time we shared with him; and he has, I suppose, done us the compliment of implying we belong. And reminded us that the sun is westering.

The martins that nest on the south wall of the house have finished their second brood, and have decided that summer

Out of Reach

is over. They have flown south with the yellowing of the leaf, and the sun slants through the willows, now towering over the river where once I fished. Their airy cages of branches still catch and dandle the light as they did when Antonia in her pram gazed up at them and gurgled. (Was it joy?) But her tree, the birch I planted when she was born, is now a big tree, and she, and her brother too, have flown the nest. Their tide is running now, as ours did once. The garden holds its memories still, memories that reach back through Antonia's wedding to all the little dramas of our lives here - my father, on his first visit, sitting beaming under the elm with a pint of his son's homebrew; losing Antonia and finding her happy in the sty with Albert's pigs; Jenny bringing Justin home the first time. (The dog, jealous of this addition to his world, went upstairs and brought Antonia's doll down and laid it at Jenny's feet.) Amid all the other tokens of pain and pleasure, our growing together like the trunks of two old trees, so that you cannot tell which is which: vine and elm creased together. But the garden is empty now as the leaves begin to fall. The apples are picked, the rucksacks are packed. Time to go, soon.

The things of which memory is made swim inconsequentially up to the surface of the mind in unguarded moments - things that acquire a significance that is as palpable and personal as it is incommunicable. The 'telephone bird', a starling which learned to imitate the phone, and (I am sure) enjoyed driving us all mad for two whole years. The cats, starting with Tailless the Manx, who adopted us in our first winter and had a happy and productive life, bringing just about a hundred attractive kittens into the world. (One of them was Short, twin to Lewis, who, brought up by the labrador, was convinced he was a dog and used to come shooting. He used to jump out at passing birds from the elm tree, and look surprised when it did not work.) Mysterious Nero, 37 inches from tip of tail to tip of nose, black as the Ace of Spades, turned up from nowhere, sleek but ravenous, one New Year's Eve. In permanent gratitude, he caught pheasants, ate a portion of the breast, and left the rest under the window for us. Last and laziest of them all, Hodge, who sat outside the wire of the hen-run and watched the rats eat the hens' food. (Occasionally he would catch an obviously geriatric rat.) A greener ring in the grass of the lawn, a little hillock, marks his favourite basking spot: there stood the elm tree my father sat under, which died in the elm disease epidemic. The bees fed on the sap that came from the flight holes, and the honey, for some reason, fermented: you could smell it without opening the hive. (That was the end of those bees. I suppose they had not too unpleasant a death, perhaps, in a cold winter hive.)

Memory clouds the sight of the present. I look out from the windows I put in twenty years ago on a street that leads back the way I have come. Else's white cottage still half turns from the road, and each year her busy little body paints it afresh, a little more slowly. Seth's sheds have long been firewood. The big barn - we saw a great gale take its roof years ago - is now two expensively converted dwellings. The poplar Colin planted is now towering over what was his paddock; the nettlebed of Len's garden is tamed into cupressus-fringed order. What was Reg's house has a new chimney, and the windows which decades of cobwebs silvered like cataracts now sparkle at the setting sun. My window once framed a quieter world, when tractors were smaller, slower, much less noisy, when trailers did not shake the house as they went past, when children could safely play in the road, go-carting on orange boxes and old pram wheels salvaged from the dump (where they were not supposed to go): down the hill and round our corner, without a thought for tomorrow. But brush away these daydreams, the cobwebs of the mind: what is our afternoon is someone else's morning. This is not the village we knew, but the one we have helped, without intending it, to shape: 'For good or ill, let the wheel turn.'

The village has just clubbed together to buy land to plant as woodland and a hundred people of all colours and accents turned up to plant the saplings on the hill where the clunch used to be quarried. The pipistrelle bats that have a breeding roost in my eaves are counted and noted each year - forty

Out of Reach

years ago, groups of 'grads' from Cambridge came and shot bats for sport as they hawked along the river in the dusk - or so I have been told. The abandoned plough along the droveway has been exhumed from the knotty entrails of the dead elm tree, and now, painted in the pale aerial blue once favoured by Ransomes, its maker, sits on a lawn, a decoration never to be used. My next-door neighbour is up in Scotland on Rhum, studying the deer, which he loves as if he were their father. A car comes down the hill: another neighbour back from New York. It was Helsinki last month. Opposite, the Mercedes is being loaded up for a trip to the Dordogne. Michael, grown-up now, goes past with his big Polish tractor, his children on the trailer behind. The eldest boy can already manage the little tractor. His father Alvah, very bent now, still cycles back home for his dinner. Where the piggery was - we used to be able to hear the pink gilts, and the sows with their little piglets, squealing and quarrelling, as we lay in bed - he has built himself a smart new house. The pigs now live in a modern pig unit at the top of the hill, and no longer each Friday when the wind is in the west do we get the sweet and sour reek of their sties being cleared out. Through the open door, I can hear Simon and Dave chatting: they are having problems with the new computer programme Simon has written. Graham goes past with his elderly labrador, rescued from the Animal Shelter: he is probably going to make a film about the village. Someone - so rumour has it - is writing a book.

A different place: the one we knew is glimpsed as at the tail of the eye, and we wish we had noticed more, and could talk across the years with those for whom we had only half an ear. But we have now become the ones who tell the Mariner's tale, while others pace past us into the hall. In this journey, always arriving, always departing, always becoming, there are no second chances. . . . Full memory - stop the world! - remains stubbornly out of reach.

I cannot reach it; and my striving eye,
Dazzles at it, as at eternity.

Epilogue

We did not, after all, leave: there seemed, in the end, despite the earnest taking stock and making of 'sensible' plans for the future, no point. The empty nest became more comfortable – unrecognisably so, when we remember the winter wind whistling under the slates as we lay abed, or the courage having a bath in winter used to demand. Over the years the fledglings returned from their far nests, bringing with them their own nestlings, and the house took them in, their voices awaking its memories. Again, in season, the summer noise of the bickering of children in the garden, marking out their space, is to be heard. (And occasional harmony.) Once more there is an outbreak of hippolatry: only this time there are two leggy blonde girls, not just one, making horse noises round the garden and populating the stable with a string of wholly imaginary but utterly real steeds of impeccable pedigree. Two boys, not just one, are learning to shoot and fish and contemplate disreputable pursuits. And for all four, their too brief times in this place will be in their memory as when every day was summer. Like their parents, they have never known a time when there were not Moseleys in Reach: four generations have known this house, and we have lived in it longer than anyone since it was built.

But… 'change in the village': when was it ever not so? The Reach the grandchildren love and will remember in their ways is not the Reach of their parents as that was not the Reach of our young selves. That is a truism. But the last decade or so has seen something much deeper than mere incremental change, imperceptible as it happens and radical only in hindsight. It has seen a revolution, conscious, visible, irresistible.. The survivors of the 'Old Village' are few and getting fewer, and their children and grandchildren have

Out of Reach

almost all left the work on the land and sought the regularity and the addictive diversions of the town. And may have had no choice but to do so. The houses are among the priciest in the county. Many of the gardens that slovens let grow nettles and others turned into models of vegetable orderliness have had building plots carved out of them. Its population is overwhelmingly middle class professional, internationally minded and travelled, and the village's entry on the Web in Upmystreet.com indicates its affluence. Reach has its own website. But many who now live here have never ventured down the Fen, have no inkling of how the slow alchemy of the seasons turns soil and water and sunlight and seed into golden harvest and unlovely sugar beet. Tractors have become huge threatening roaring monsters, capable of speeds higher than those claimed for our first car, the Hillman with the headlight held on by string and putty, which brought our few belongings here. The surviving little Fergusons and Fordsons – they were not 'little' *then* – are collectors' items, and come out, looking tiny, for ploughing matches with their engines polished and gleaming in fresh paint: and just occasionally one gets on the winter wind that curious smell of paraffin and petrol that melts away the decades between us and those early winters then we watched the tumbling gulls following the plough as it laboured through the thick land on the hill. For the first time in the village's 4000 (or more) year history, its life and economy owe virtually nothing to the land on which it stands. None of the wealth is created here or won from the Fen The waterway that made it grow in the first place is now just the haunt of coot and her'n, its reeds occasionally brushed in summer by a chugging holiday boat. There are signs by the sewage works (which now 'polishes', as Anglian Water calls it, the effluent from several villages before discharging it into the Lode) reminding the passer-by who has reached this *ne plus ultra* of the port that once was here. In this disarticulation from our common past, the past of our very race, our generation is entering on known territory. The pessimist in me suspects we may be living on borrowed time.

The biggest changes are down the Fen. For some years, in

Out of Reach

one of the worst bits of legal vandalism for quick profit in my whole experience, much of the best land in Europe was mined for turf to patch golf courses and create instant lawns. When there was not much left to mine, the turf merchant sold huge tracts to the National Trust, which intends to establish a tongue of wetland and marsh along the river from Wicken Fen to Cambridge. There is a lot of persuasive talk about amenity, wildlife, and leisure activities, and the project has mightily divided the communities that are affected. A lot of money has been spent, not all of it wisely: planting trees at the wrong time so that they die does not encourage confidence in the capabilities of the overseers of the 'vision', and several thousand pounds have been spent on elaborate gates and on concrete mounting blocks beside them, blocks which will greatly puzzle any future archaeologists. (We used to be able to mount a horse without a block, but perhaps times have changed. *Nous avons changé tout cela...*) Where unease does seem justified is in seeing the land won so hardly and at such cost of human toil from the waters and the waste for the feeding of the children of men deliberately turned back to weeds and wilderness and wet. This does not feel like keeping faith with the old folk. But perhaps the game is even deeper, as sea levels rise and the inevitability of a North Sea surge that will one day top the flood banks of the Wash is accepted. There is no better defence against the energy of the tide than wetland. And the Cam, as is always forgotten, is by nature tidal at least as far up as Waterbeach: I knew a man who was taken as a child in 1920 to see a particularly high tide come up the Cam in a miniscule tidal bore. One day – perhaps, indeed, very long hence - the stream at the bottom of my garden will be brackish, and the rich fen the haunt of seals and orcs and sea mews' clang.

Some changes are hugely welcome, aesthetically at least. The slope of Reach Hill is now plotted by hedges and sheep may safely graze after an absence of three generations of men. And their meat is welcome on our table. Many trees have been planted, and are maturing well. The old clunch pits have been planted into one of the most lovely new woods I

Out of Reach

have seen, partly by the Woodland Trust and partly by village effort. The wild cherry is hung with Housman's snow in season, and the spindle tree flaunts its flashy colours between the sombre shades of the yews. Deer and badgers share the evening. Nightingales used to sing decades ago down in the unkempt bits of the Fen, and then disappeared. But they are now back, singing in the little trees to the silent stars, and we can hear Philomela bewail her plight from dusk to dawn from our bedroom. The wood and its clearings have brought back the blue butterflies, and the moths, and a host of little creatures have moved in whom one catches in the corner of the eye, sometimes, as one walks the dog. And there are still moments as golden as any recalled in the earlier chapters of this book. My daughter's son and I went up with the dog in the June gloaming to hear the nightingales which he had never heard, and though the gloom we glimpsed another lad, about Tom's age, and his father the shepherd (he is a teacher really, but what is the difference?) making their way up the dark lane towards us. Courtesies, and chat, and then companionable silence as we waited for the show to begin in the bushes below the big ash tree. But then the noise of an engine, and along the hilltop track in his unlit Jeep slowly comes young Mick, who once had a tame jackdaw and used to play with Justin. His son is beside him and the rifle with which they have been rabbiting is along the dashboard. More chat and pleasantries... and not a nightingale to be heard. But Gareth takes out his mobile phone, into which he has programmed many bird's songs, and plays the song of a nightingale...And all Heaven breaks loose as every nightingale for acres around joins in. Tom will remember the song of the nightingale, and a golden evening.

In a little clearing in the wood, all of a sudden one June the ground was carpeted with bee orchids, not the commonest of flowers. The oldest people in the village took our surprise

Out of Reach

with some amusement, for they remembered them growing there long before the silent springs of the '50s and '60s. Perhaps they had been simply waiting... perhaps the animals wait, the land itself waits, until our brief hour is done. Just so, beneath the towns, beneath the present, the fields like memory lie sleeping underneath.